UWE PETERSEN

Unconventional Consideration Manners of the Economic Crisis III

What is to be done as a solution for the crisis?

PL ACADEMIC RESEARCH

Bibliographic Information published by the Deutsche Nationalbibliothek
The Deutsche Nationalbibliothek lists this publication in the Deutsche Nationalbibliografie; detailed bibliographic data is available in the internet at http://dnb.d-nb.de.

Cover Design: © Olaf Gloeckler, Atelier Platen, Friedberg

Library of Congress Cataloging-in-Publication Data

Petersen, Uwe, 1932-
[Unkonventionelle Betrachtungsweisen zur Wirtschaftskrise III. English]
Unconventional consideration manners of the economic crisis III : what is to be done as a solution for the crisis? / Uwe Petersen. — 1 Edition.
pages cm
Includes bibliographical references.
ISBN 978-3-631-64314-3
1. Financial crises. 2. Economic policy. 3. Financial institutions—Government policy. I. Title.
HB3722.P46813 2013
339.5—dc23

2013016086

ISBN 978-3-631-64314-3 (Print)
E-ISBN 978-3-653-03269-7 (E-Book)
DOI 10.3726/978-3-653-03269-7

PL Academic Research is an Imprint of Peter Lang GmbH.

Peter Lang – Frankfurt am Main · Bern · Bruxelles · New York · Oxford · Warszawa · Wien

www.peterlang.de

Contents

Introduction

This book is a little modified and actualised translation of "*Unkonventionelle Betrachtungsweisen zur Wirtschaftskrise III. Was ist zur Lösung der Krise zu tun?" published in German in 2012.*

In the book *"Wirtschaftsethik und Wirtschaftspolitik. Zur Überwindung der globalen Wirtschaftskrise. Von der liberalen zur sozialliberalen Wirtschaftsordnung"* [*Economic Ethics and Economic Policy. For Overcoming the Global Economic Crisis. From Liberal to the Social-liberal Economic System*"][11], published in May, 2010, the present economic crisis was derived from the development of the economic-ethical norms, and the economic behavioural manners, economic maxims and possible solutions for overcoming the crisis were indicated. Moreover it becomes clear that the resulted dislocations of the economic system have become so big that they can no longer be settled with conventional economic measures.

Then in the beginning of 2011 as it were for the hasty reader, the book "*Unkonventionelle Betrachtungsweisen zur Wirtschaftskrise. Von Haien, Heuschrcken und anderem Getier" [Unconventional Consideration Manners of the Economic Crisis I. From Sharks, Grasshoppers and other Creatures]* was published which explained aphoristically succinct aspects of the economic crisis. But the single analyses nevertheless, together provide a whole understanding.

At the end of August, 2011, the second volume of the "*Unkonventionelle Betrachtungsweisen zur Wirtschaftskrise II. Krankheiten des Wirtschaftssystems und Möglichkeiten und Grenzen ihrer Heilung" [Unconventional Consideration Manners of the Economic Crisis II] appeared,* which exemplarily analyses and describes the economic case history of single countries "*Illnesses of the Economic System and Possibilities and Limits of their Healing*".

Because the conventional economic measures shown turn out insufficient, fight only symptoms and only shift the problems one thinks of the present solution attempts of the indebtedness crises of European states which only shift the debt and also endanger with it, in the end, the creditworthiness of the remaining states in this third volume of the "*Consideration Manners of the Economic Crisis III. What is to be done for the Solution of the Crisis?*" unconventional solution possibilities of the financial crisis and economic crisis are indicated, and are backed up ethically.

Also the treatises in this volume are clear for themselves, and at the same time give an overview about the crisis problems all together, and that's why it seemed to be justified to translate only this volume in English.

---

1 Petersen (2010a) Publisher Dr. Kovac Hamburg. 441 pages.

A. The axiomatic and economic-ethical bases of our today's finance-capitalistic economic system and their relation to the sense of economy[2]

Economy was understood by the Greeks as an order enclosing the people; but from the Jews, however, as a remedial event escorted by God two views which became effective in Europe. Hence, to the understanding of the European economic development and the European economic understanding it makes sense to show both these views first.

I. Economy as an order enclosing the people

H. Raven writes: >>for the whole old-European world "Economy" means the household of a man or a married couple of status (with slaves or servants), as well as the regular equipment and management of the same. The second vocabulary part (-nomina) refers to the distribution and management as a continuous structure of the right (distributive justice) of the economy and the political system [3]. From here, it is to be understood that the word connection "oiko-nom" has been often used from the outset for organisation problems and problems of utilisation, also beyond the sphere of the house [4].<<[5]

>>*Aristotle* treats the economy in the first part of the «politics», because the polity itself is a community existing of several villages, and the village a summary of several houses (οἰκίαι) [6]. Because the person is by his nature ζῷον πολιτικόν, a being relying on community and the single person in this respect cannot live self-sufficiently, the state is by its nature as a whole more original than its parts, therefore, also more than the housing association or the single citizen; the state represents a completely self-sufficient community and allows thus the existence of a domestic community, because the domestic as well as the political community fulfil their sense only in view of the general telos of the «good life». However, besides, the economic autarky of the master of the house is also valid vice versa as the condition of his participation in the public life of free town citizens [7].<<[8]

---

[2] The text of this chapter exists extensively of extracts from my book *Economic Ethics and Economic Policy*, Petersen (2010a), p. 314 following.

[3] E. LAROCHE: Hist. de la racine NEMen grec ancien (Paris 1949) 142–144 translated from German.

[4] loc. cit.. 141.

[5] H. Rabe: *Ökonomie*, in : HWPh Vol. 6, P. 1149 translated from German.

[6] ARISTOTELES, Pol. I, 2, 1252 b translated from German.

[7] loc. cit.1253 a.

[8] H. Rabe: *Ökonomie*, in : HWPh Vol. 6, P. 1149.

How everything hangs together with all in an *ecological top* and causes itself mutually, thus also in an *economy as* understood in the original sense. Also what we understand by an *economic* behaviour, is already incorporated in the early concept of *Economy*, indeed, in the form that everything must stand in the right measure to each other. Who acts in this sense economically, acts at the same time *virtuously*.

Rabe writes :>>The signs of the natural unity, the given telos and the clever effectiveness make housekeeping an art which knowledge Xenophon and Aristotle call a virtue. Thus beside ethics and politics, the economy in the Aristotle tradition makes up the third part of the practical philosophy.<<[9]

In a totality there are no unnecessary components, and therefore also no waste. Everything is attuned with each other. The single person does not face this original economy, but is a part of it. After Aristotle's understanding the economy also encloses the management of the house, whose objects are the use of the tools as well as the instructions of the slaves, beside the description of the social relations [[10]].<<[11]

If however one understands economy as households in this original sense, >>it is doubtful whether the art of acquisition (κτητική) is still to be understood as a part of the economy; for: «One brings, the other uses» [[12]]. However, the "natural" art of acquisition, which is bringing the things necessary for the household through work and hunt and not by exchange, corresponds to the nature and the economy. The easy barter turns out acceptable with the sense of household when it is pursued as an exchange by consumer durables between the single households, and serves thus for the guarantee of the natural autarky of the Oikos.<<[13]

If the barter leaves this frame and becomes trade with the aim to gain profit, the good exchange falls out of the economy. Then it is no longer about equal giving and taking within the scope of a closed housekeeping.

This becomes even clearer with the transition to the money economy because money is of no value when used for itself. At most it could be accepted as a means of bartering, but not as the value of itself which still increases with interest. Accordingly the money economy does not belong to the *economy* any more, according to Aristotle. Rabe writes: >>The resulted convention to take money instead of goods allows... the businessman's art (Chrematistic) [[14]] which seems to know no more borders of the acquisition of wealth[[15]]. The "pure interest" business and "usury" is most despicable, «that which earns directly from the

---

[9] H. Rabe, loc. cit.

[10] Aristoteles, Pol. I, 4, 1253 b 23–38.

[11] H. Rabe, loc. cit.., p. 1149f.

[12] Aristoteles, Pol. I, 8, 1256 a 11.

[13] H. Rabe, loc. cit.., p. 1150.

[14] Aristoteles, Pol. I, 8, 1256 b 34–37.

[15] Aristoteles, Pol. I, 9, 1257 a 29.

money and not from that for which the money is used» [[16]]. Aristotle excludes this kind of monetary acquisition not only from the economy, but from an ethical point of view, considers is as – measured in the principle of «compensatory justice» which, when measured within the scope of the ethics as the fair in the exchange – he determines to be untenable. The barter can only take place on the basis of the equality because, otherwise, the advantage of one would imply the imposition of the other [[17]]. <<[18]

Accordingly Aristotle also treats the money economy as an art separated from the economy. >>From here [as Rabe writes] two different approaches of the economy, within the history of the practical philosophy, take their starting point which orientate themselves on the one hand on the constitution of a household, and on the other hand on the market-related working life.<<[19] However, the general principle for ethical behaviour remains furthermore as the all-embracing *economy* in which the individuals are only limbs.

As Rabe writes, you find the separation of economy and chrematistic in >>all traditional constitutions with their countless "police" orders. Correspondingly the commercial processing of agricultural products can belong to the economy only when the producer is entitled to it due to his social status, and the products serve his own use. Everything beyond that is chrematistic, craft or market orientated activity, which are subjected to privileging, and thus to the management and control of the community and the authority (court of oikos lords). The well-organised management of this economic practice is a science, which A. de MONTCHRESTIEN 1615 (for the first time in the title of a state economic investigation) calls «political economy». It assumes the possession of regalia which belong only to a town state or a highly princely economy, as generally the estates determine the structure of any economy.<<[20]

Respectively, the *economy* widens with it to the town state and then to a state of estates controlled by kings and princes and, finally, to *Mercantilism*. Accordingly A. Seigfried writes: >>Parallelizing house management and state management, and the treatment of state-economic and national-economic questions, is characteristic for the whole older development of the political economy or «économie politique patronale» [[21]]. It is not only the adjustment of all economic questions on the eudemonic welfare politics and the power increase of the nation state that is typical, but also the same equation of the princely regency with the position of a landlord and the national commercial economy

---

16 Aristoteles, Pol. I, 10, 1258 b 1–8.

17 Eth. Nic. V, 5–8, 1130 b–1133 b 29.

18 H. Rabe: *Ökonomie*, in : HWPh Vol. 6, p. 1150.

19 loc. cit..

20 loc. cit.

21 T. FUNCK-BRENTANO, *L'économie politique patronale* = Einl. zur Neu-A. von MONTCHRESTIEN, Traicté de l'œconomie politique (Rouen 1615) (Paris 1930) I–CXVII.

with the princely household. In this view the absolutistic economy is first orientated to the "Camera", the «treasury and tax authority» of the prince, and later to the "municipal economy" and the town economy and land economy, and is still an integral moment of the state management and as such even just a part of the 'politics'. For the political power of the mercantilist state has the economic independence of own territorial economy and national economy to its condition, the economic balance of the balances of trade corresponds to the political balance of the European state system, which not only appeared guaranteed to the English Mercantilists and French economic politicians, but also to the German and Austrian Cameralists – and thus by a restrictive commercial policy concerning the import of industrial ready products and the exportation of raw materials and precious metals [22].<<[23]

That is: >>The subdivision of the economy having becoming current into the economy of the prince and the economy of the private individuals [24] or in «private» and the «state economy» [25] already refers to the fact that with the emancipation of the family and the sovereign monarch from estates based society and its mediation by the modern traffic society, the old-European concept of the economy has also now accepted two different meanings. But also the new concept of the economy is still related in this respect to the tradition as it results from transference of the model of the household on the "Camera" of the prince and, finally, on the whole state. Thus it paves the way for a state economy or 'political economy'different of the house economy but nevertheless, still rooted in the traditional way of thinking.<<[26]

Economic activities are still also interpreted at times of Mercantilism from a comprehensive consideration of the national economy, and not from the intention of the singles to make profit. Even Adam Smith still argues in such a way as Seigfried reports: >>with "Wealth of nations", appeared in 1776, SMITH has resolved to show the political economy as a part of the «science of a states-man and legislator» in the form of an independent branch of the moral philosophy [27]. In his definition of this science at the beginning of the 4th book, it appears how much he is also still obliged to the traditional political reference framework: «Political economy considered as a branch of the science of a statesman or legislator proposes two distinct objects. ... It proposes to enrich both the people and the sovereign» [28]. Thus the 'politics' must be also looked about as a starting

[22] Though polemic, very illuminating. J. H. G. JUSTI: *Die Chimäre des Gleichgewichts von Europa* (1758); generally K. PRIBRAM: *Die Idee des Gleichgewichts in der älteren nationalökon. Theorie.* Z. Volkswirtschaft, Sozialpolitik und Verwaltung 17 (1908) 1–28.

[23] A. Seigfried: *Politische Ökonomie*, in : HWPh Vol.. 6, p. 1165f.

[24] J. G. WALCH: Art. ‹Ö.›, in: Philop. Lex. 3 (41775) 312.

[25] W. T. KRUG: Art. ‹Oekonomik›, in: Handwb. der philop. Wisp. 3 (21833) 97.

[26] H. Rabe: *Ökonomie*, in : HWPh Vol. 6, P. 1151f.

[27] *An inquiry into the nature and causes of the wealth of nations* (London 1776).

[28] loc. cit. Buch IV, P. 1.

point of the theory of the national wealth developed by Smith; he not only still identifies in traditional wise wealth with power [[29]], but also his state-economic investigations which deal with the state police and welfare police, i.e. legal care, teaching care and economic care as well as the military being, as opposed to the analysis of the original reasons and the distribution of the economical wealth (revenue), and takes up the whole space of the extensive 5th book of "Wealth of nations".<<[30]

>>Only D. RICARDO sees a purely positively proceeding natural-legal science in the political economy, which is to be kept free from all political and natural-juridical connotations. A letter place directed against SMITH and TH. R. MALTHUS, in which he pleads for the consideration of market price fixing and distribution processes to be separated from moral theology and the economic value theory coming from modern natural law, is informative for the self image of the economic theory in England and France during the whole 19. Cent: «You think political economy is an enquiry into the nature and causes of wealth: I think it should rather be called an enquiry into the laws which determine the division of the produce of industry amongst the classes who concur in its formation» [[31]].<<[32]

With the scientification of the economy, economic theory becomes like the means to be able to control economic phenomena, such as with natural sciences. With it, the individual comes to the fore as a reference point of economic activities.

Firstly, the cause for it is the strengthening of trade and with it the increasing political significance of the traders. Trade still also remains first within the scope of estates oriented images as it is shown, for example, by the concept of the *royal businessman*. In the course of this development economy becomes a special area which differentiates itself from the mind-set, from the culture, the judicial system and also the politics. Economic activities only serve to function towards the real life of men; up to that economic activity is only a procurement of the necessary livelihood.

Work is only regarded as drudgery. The real life is consumption. So, work loses its intrinsic value, especially according to liberal free-enterprise understanding. And in itself, it is also no longer virtuous, self-adequate or even an expression of self-realisation. If one would include these aspects in the assessment of work, then i.e. heavy-duty work or the work of cleaning ladies would have to be paid higher, than work of managers or even speculators.

After this understanding a person himself feels *opposed* to the economy, and *economic* becomes *rational* action with reference to *self-imposed goals*.

---

29 II, Kap. 5.

30 A. Seigfried: *Politische Ökonomie*, in : HWPh Vol. 6, P. 1168.

31 D. RICARDO see Letters of D. Ricardo to Th. R. Malthus, hg. J. BONAR (Oxford 1887) 175; see also D. RICARDO: *On the principles of pol. economy and taxation* (London 1817) Introd.

32 A. Seigfried: *Politische Ökonomie*, in : HWPh Vol. 6, P. 1168.

II. Economy as a remedial process escorted by God

Up to now we have only looked at practical economic work from the view of antique tradition, an aspect which is of course continuing as effect and which also, according to liberal understanding, does not award work a special rank as such. However, the dynamism of European economy is not understandable without including the Jewish / Christian inheritance as a motivation for economic activity.

With Christianity, and the idea of an empire of God enclosing everything, the economy also gets a new foundation. U. Dierse writes: >>In theology "economy" (Greek οἰκονομία = οἰ; lat. dispositio, but often also: dispensatio) is a basic concept of remedial-historical thinking. Although in the 2nd Century B.C., *Polybios* had already conceived history as a «general and comprehensive economy of the events» (τὴν καθόλου καὶ συλλήβδην οἰ. τῶν γεγονότων), [33], the concept is not understood as a connection with a common aim by the early Fathers of the Church, yet is historically unambiguous. ‹Economy› is called in this connection first ‹plan›, ‹decision› of God. Also of the profane Hellenistic broad usage (good conduct and management: οἰ. καὶ διοίκησις [34]; order of the universe and all things: ἡ τῶν ὅλων οἰ. [35]) is still present and works in the Judaism (Philon: God as a ruler, οἰκονόμος of the universe [36]), in the Gnosis (...), in the hermetic literature (God is «dispensator distributorque bonorum», the sun is «vitae dispensator») [37] and, finally, in the early Christianity, so possibly when *Tatian* called the human body and the universe as a κατ' οἰ. συμφωνίας ἁρμονία, *Theophilus of Antioch* praises the 6 day's work of the creation as οἰ., *Clemens of Alexandria* praises the wise equipment of the world by God (...) or *Origines* says that all being takes the rank being due to him in the coming world order (in ordinatione ac dispensatione mundi) [38]. In the New Testament οἰκονόμος and οἰ. first appear in the parable of the clever but unfair house supervisor [39]. *Paulus* transfers οἰ. on the management of the apostolic office [40]. The οἰκονόμος is «house holder of the secrets of God» and his mercy gifts [41].

---

33 POLYBIOS I, 4, 3.

34 EPIKTET, Disp. III, 24, 92; 14, 7; see EPIKUR, Ep. 1. Epicurea, hg. H. USENER (1887, ND 1966) 29.

35 CHRYSIPP, SVF 2, 269. 273. 338; see CELSUS in ORIGENES, C. Celp. VIII, 53; as well as XENOPHON, Memor. IV, 3, 13.

36 PHILON, De conf. ling. 98; see De decal. 53; De op. mundi 11. 54; De Jop. 192; De Abrah. 69.

37 HERMES TRISMEGISTUS, Asclep. 27. 29f., hg. A. D. NOCK 2 (Paris 1960) 332. 337.

38 TATIAN, Or. ad Graec. XII, hg. E. SCHWARTZ (1888) 13; THEOPHILUS VON ANTIOCHIEN, Ad. Autol. II, 12, hg. G. BARDY (Paris 1948) = Sources chrétiennes (= SC) 20, 130; ORIGENES, De princ. I, 6, 2.

39 Luk. 12, 42; 16, 1ff.

40 1 Kor. 9, 17; Kol. 1, 25; Eph. 3, 2.

41 1 Kor. 4, 1f.; Tit. 1, 7; see 1 Petr. 4, 10.

Above all, however, oi. means the decision of God, his remedial plan which Christ is carrying out in the fullness of the times [42]. (It is not clear whether oi. in 1 Tim. 1, 4 also means the divine decision, or rather the education of men in faith.) <<[43]

>>With the Fathers of the Church the concept finds wide response. *Ignatius* and other early apologists [[44]] speak of the remedial event which refers to Christ and is realised by him [[45]].The letter to *Diognet* reproaches to the Jews an arbitrary view of oi., the divine plans [[46]].With *Justinus* oi. means the world Government and providence of God which also possibly appears with incidents incomprehensible in itself of the Old Testament [[47]], as well as the realisation of the remedial plan of Christ [[48]] as well as single remedial processes (incarnation,suffering and death of Christ) [[49]].The concept then receives another further active meaning with *Tatian*. Here oi. is the inner-Trinitarian process, the development of the logo from God, which with the concept oi. is interpreted not as a complete separation, but as an economic division, as lighting a torch in another [[50]].<<[51]

>>Very often and in a different sense oi. / dispositio appears *with Irenäus of Lyons*. Beside ‹(creation) order›, ‹world plan›, ‹decision›, ‹arrangement› of God oi. means above all the remedial plan, as a whole as well as in its single events. The Christians should investigate the mysterious remedial order, and understand the aim and intention of God with the humanity (τὴν πραγματείαν καὶ τὴν oi. τοῦ θεοῦ) [[52]]. The Gnostic and Heretic misjudge the remedial plan and alters oi. [[53]].

---

42 Eph. 1, 10; 3, 9.

43 U. Dierse: *Ökonomie*, in : HWPh Vol. 6, P. 1153.

44 ARISTIDES, Apol., hg. E. HENNECKE (1893) 9; ATHENAGORAS, Lib. pro christ., hg. E. SCHWARTZ (1891) 25.

45 IGNATIUS VON ANTIOCHIEN, Ep. ad Eph. XX, 1; see XVIII, 2, hg. TH. CAMELOT. SC 10 (Paris 41969) 76. 74.

46 Ep. ad Diognetum IV, 5, hg. H.-I. MARROU. SC 33a (Paris 21965) 60.

47 JUSTINUS, Dial. c. Tryph. CVII, 3; CXXXIV, 2; CXLI, 4. MPG 6, 725. 785. 800; prepared already by MARC AUREL XI, 18; IV, 19. 51 (oi. as clever secondary aims and calculation) and with PHILON, Quaest. gen. (nur armen, erhalten): Jakobs Lie under the compulsion of the circumstances; see J. REUMANN: Oi. as 'ethical accommodation in the fathers, in: Studia Patristica 3, hg. F. L. CROSS (Berlin 1961) 370–379; B. BOTTE: Oikonomia. Quelques emplois spécifiquement chrétiens, in: Corona gratiarum. Misc. patr., hist. et liturg. E. DEKKERS ... oblata (Brügge/Den Haag 1975) 1, 3–9.

48 JUSTINUS, loc. cit. LXVII, 6; LXXXVII, 5. MPG 6, 629. 684.

49 loc. cit. XXX, 3; XXXI, 1; XLV, 4; LXVII, 6; CIII, 3; CXX, 1. MPG 6, 540. 573. 629. 717. 753.

50 TATIAN, Or. ad Graec. V, loc. cit. [6] 5f.

51 U. Dierse: *Ökonomie*, in : HWPh Vol. 6, P. 1153f.

52 IRENÄUS VON LYON, Adv. haer., hg. A. ROUSSEAU u.a. II, 28, 1 = SC 294, 270; see II, 4, 1 = 294, 44; II, 25, 3 = 294, 254; I, 10, 3 = 264, 162; IV, 7, 4 = 100, 464; V, 10, 1 = 153, 125

The spirit of God governs the history from the beginning up to the end in different economies (from initio usque ad finem variis dispositionibus), and always stands by the human race [[54]]. Therefore, the typological interpretation of the Old Testament becomes necessary: the prophets have their value advance interpreting at the New Testament in the remedial economy [[55]].They themselves cannot yet recognise the orders of God and facilities of the redemption in their full meaning. To them, God is only indistinct and mysterious [[56]]. For the remedial plan only becomes obvious with Christ who passes it and brings it to completion (veniens by universam dispositionem et omnia in semetipsum recapitulans) [[57]].Thus oi. especially calls the remedial work of Christ (dispositio salutis nostrae) [[58]], which is «recapitulation», fulfilment of the events prefigured in the Old Testament and summary of the single remedial events of God [[59]]. The incarnation in particular is a fact of the remedial economy [[60]], and also the cross death [[61]] and other events of the New Testament [[62]].In the arrival of Christ the new remedial economy of the freedom (nova libertatis dispositio) is founded as a detachment of the old alliance of servitude [[63]]. In an education of the people to a perfection where bad and evil also has its value, God has determined everything for the realisation and revelation of his remedial orders (ad manifestationem dispositionum) [[64]]. In that respect economy appears only at a place in connection with the Trinity, and also means economy of redemption [[65]].<<[66]

This reinterpretation of the economy matters to the advancement of the remedial events. It gives a remedial-historical dimension to the economic action, with which the person can define himself first as an executor of the divine will.

---

[53] IRENÄUS VON LYON, Adv. haer., hg. A. ROUSSEAU u.a. I, 16, 3 = SC 264, 262; III, 12, 12 = 211, 235; 111, 16, 8= 211, 319; 111, 24, 1 = 211, 471; IV, 1, 1 = 100, 395; V, 2, 2= 153, 31; V, 13, 2= 153, 169; V, 19, 2 = 153, 251.

[54] III, 12, 13 = SC 211, 236; IV, 33, 1 = 100, 802; IV, 28, 2 = 100, 758; IV, 33, 7 = 100, 818.

[55] IV, 33, 10 = SC 100, 824; IV, 31, 1 = 100, 788.

[56] IV, 20, 8. 10f. = SC 100, 652. 656. 660; IV, 21, 3 = 100, 684.

[57] III, 16, 6 = SC 211, 312; III, 23, 1 = 211, 444.

[58] III, 1, 1 = SC 211, 20; III, 13, 1 = 211, 252; III, 18, 2 = 211, 344; III, 22, 3 = 211, 438; IV, prol. 4 = 100, 390.

[59] V, 20, 2 = SC 153, 260; V, 23, 2 = 153, 290.

[60] III, 16, 3 = SC 211, 300; III, 17, 4 = 211, 338; V, 14, 2 = 153, 188; V, 20, 1 = 153, 254.

[61] III, 18, 5 = SC 211, 354; IV, 5, 5 = 100, 434; V, 17, 4 = 153, 232.

[62] I, 10, 1 = SC 264, 154; IV, 23, 1f. = 100, 694. 696; IV, 26, 1 = 100, 714; V, 19, 2 = 153, 252.

[63] III, 10, 5 = SC 211, 134; see III, 10, 2 = 211, 120.

[64] IV, 37, 7 = SC 100, 942.

[65] Epid. 47, hg. L. M. FROIDEVAUX. SC 62 (Paris 1959) 106.

[66] U. Dierse: *Ökonomie*, in : HWPh Vol. 6, P. 1154.

For >>the person stands, according to the historian *Orosius*, as God's creature under his management (dispensatio); God steers and governs the world [[67]] with wise providence.<<[68]

In the course of the re-strengthening of the individualistic antique mentality in the Renaissance, and later the Age of Enlightenment, by this Christian impulse the person himself becomes the reference point of further world development. Divine remedial events become the *progress faith*. Without this Christian remedial-historical impulse, Max of Weber's derivation of capitalistic action from the mind of Protestantism is also not understandable [[69]]. For the development of capitalism started in particular from Calvinist entrepreneurs.

According to J. Calvin, in the organisation of the alliance of His mercy, God the Lord follows >>an order (oeconomiam et ordinem) which progresses up to the full revelation of his magnificence (temporis progressu) [[70]]. God has taught his people and governs the church. The gradual revelation depends on the economy of his rule (totum pendet ex oeconomia divini regiminis) [[71]]. From this view the concept enters the federal theology which thinks historically differently before the background of a constant substance of the alliance of mercy, both time wise and applying realisation. This happens in the respective economies: Mercy and revelation are distributed in ever special degrees and forms, conform to the status and the ability to grasp of the people. The clever, systematic wisdom of God becomes apparent in His different communication to the believers according to the historical situation [[72]]. The difference and sequence of the economy of the Old and New Testament is first explained with it; then, however, one can also accept in general after time, place and human constitution varying economy and, as *Zinzendorf*, understand the difference of the denominations as an adjustment (economy) to the «country's temperature and air» [[73]]. Because the single economies stand in a sense as a full connection, there will be a successively progressing revelation of God, also below the New Testament till the end of the

---

[67] PAULUS OROSIUS, Hist. adv. pag. II, 1, hg. C. ZANGEMEISTER. CSEL 5, 81.

[68] U. Dierse: *Ökonomie*, in : HWPh Vol. 6, P. 1156.

[69] Max Weber: *Die protestantische Ethik und der Geist des Kapitalismus*

[70] J. CALVIN, *Inst. rel. christ.* II, 10, 20.

[71] Com. in Gal. IV, 1. Corpus Reform. 78, 225.

[72] A. HEIDANUS: *Corpus theol. christ.* (1686) 2, 3ff.; J. BRAUN: Doctrina foederum (21691) 414. 279; B. PICTET Theol. christ. (1696) 642ff.; J. H. HEIDEGGER: Medulla theol. Christ. (1696); H. WITSIUS: De oe. foederum Dei (21685); W. MOMMA: *De varia conditione & statu ecclesiae Dei sub triplici oe.* (1698); J. COCCEJUS: Summa doctrinae de foedere et testamento Dei (61703) c. Xf.; L. RIISSEN: Summa theol. didactico-elencticae (1703) 279; J. H. MAJUS: *Oe. temporum novi testamenti* (1708); J. W. PETERSEN: Jesus Christus ... nach seinen vielfältigen Oe. (1721); J. F. BUDDEUS: Compendium inst. theol. christ. (1748) 456f.

[73] A. HEIDANUS, loc. cit.; N. VON ZINZENDORF zit. bei O. UTTENDÖRFER: Zinzendorfs Weltbetrachtung (1929) 79; P. BAUMGARTEN, Vorrede zu G. ARNOLD: *Wahre Abbildung der ersten Christen* (61740); G. B. BILFINGER: *Varia in fasciculos collecta* (1743) 2, 229.

times [74]. Thus the epochs of history are connected to a totality; passed by the «bonitas of Christ» in different stadia (diversas dispensationes) from childhood up to manhood [75]. *J. A. Bengel* derives the basic idea that in the «Holy Writing the big household of God leading His people by His words and works is described » [76] as a complete chronology of world history, from the creation up to the Last Judgment [77].<<[78] As a Christian inheritance the idea *of progress* remains furthermore connected with the sense of economic action, namely so far that today one can fancy no economic action without *growth* and *progress*.

III. The European economy as a synthesis of antique and Jewish/Christian understanding of economy

If one compares antique and Jewish mentality with each other, one can characterise antique as a *lord's consciousness* and Jewish as a *knight's consciousness.* The Greek wanted to be the same to his gods and, like them, rule the phenomena of the world as a *motionless mover.* Referring to himself as the sensuousness, he wanted to control and consume them, provided that he did not move ideally in the timeless ideas which form the basis of the phenomena. This is also valid for one's own body which is made fit through sport, and of which movements are enjoyed. However, the pleasure should be steered by reason, and propagated in particular, as with *Epicure.*

Such a life can only be led of course as long as enough slaves are available for the provision of the living, and as servants are available or can be procured by wars. In this respect antique life is based on war and suppression and results, if one cannot win, in destruction.

As opposed to this, the Jews have their self in a transcendental God whom they serve actively. They do not enjoy the *present* moment like the Greeks, but hope for a *future paradise*, to which God will lead them. Greeks live in the *present*, Jews in the *future*. If both mentalities combine one with another, the self-

---

[74] see C. VITRINGA: *Anakrisis Joannis Apostoli* (1705).

[75] P. POIRET*: L'économie divine* ... (Amsterdam 1687); Oe. divinae libri sex (1705, 21728) 1, 732; see zum ganzen E. BUSCH: *Der Beitrag und Ertrag der Föderaltheol. für ein gesch. Verständnis der Offenbarung*, in: Oikonomia ..., hg. F. CHRIST, O. Cullmann zum 65. Geb. (1967) 171–190; G. SCHRENK: *Gottesreich und Bund im älteren Protestantismus* (1923) 300–307. 313f. 317.

[76] J. A. BENGEL: Weltalter (1746) 1; see bereits Bengels Lehrer J. CHR. PFÄFF: De fine oe. Christi (1713); J. W. JÄGER: *Compendium theol. positivae* (1702).

[77] BENGEL: *Ordo temporum a principio per periodos oe. divinae historicas atque propheticas ad finem usque* (1741, 21770); see CHR. A. CRUSIUS: Hypomnemata ad theologiam propheticam (1764); see M. BRECHT: J. A. Bengels Theol. der Schrift. Z. Theol. Kirche 64 (1967) 111–116.

[78] U. Dierse: *Ökonomie*, in : HWPh Vol. 6, P. 1157f.

confident antique person himself becomes a creative God who modifies the world and realises himself in it. The master referring the world on him turns back to the world and forms it after his intentions.

So philosophical deepening in the being of the phenomena becomes science which structures the phenomena in entities, and thus makes them controllable. As a result, *science* produces *inventions* after which products can be produced more rationally, and new ones can be developed.

The modern entrepreneurship, which intends the control and creation of the world, is based on this philosophy. First according to the doctrine of Calvin the early puritanical enterpriser still believes in a transcendental God, but not in any such a way that he only follows God's orders, but in such a way that he reads whether he is chosen by God or not, from the success of his actions. Then he later acts of his own volition.

IV. The liberal capitalistic economic ethics

If different ethnic groups clashed in the earliest times, they normally separated themselves from each other or even tried to destroy the other group. When it came to communication between different ethnic groups, outside of armed conflicts, it was the work of the traders. For this intercultural communication a trader had to leave his original *Oikos*.

As previously mentioned, according to *Aristotle* the original embedded being in a traditional *economy* ends with the exchange of goods with others. At most the real exchange, which is in the interest of a family because the exchanged goods are used, can still be regarded in harmony with housekeeping. However, trade without any interest in the goods but only to make profit is no more *economy* in the traditional sense.

Therefore, the great empires which are closed economies like China and Japan, have also prevented national trade for their compatriots respectively, after sea trade had developed in the Song Dynasty (960-1279) once it came to China, it was forbidden again. As far as goods from China came to the remaining world or from there to China the traders were not Chinese. The unlimited access to the Chinese and Japanese market had to be militarily forced, as everybody knows, by the European colonial powers.

Traders are already self-confident individuals. They do not act as a comprehensive community in the interest of any *economy*, but rather in their own name and interest. Hence, in the course of history they were often treated as dishonest citizens, and to a certain extent excluded from society. They only became recognised as state-weight-bearing and “respectable businessmen” in important commercial towns, where the traders had to mutually support one another and stick together because they were responsible for the order and the town life at the same time; one thinks of the *Hanseatic Towns in this regard.*

As a trader, he has no emotional respect either to his people they are only potential buyers to him or to his goods they have only commercial value to him. Although buyers and sellers still recognise the rules applying for trade and behaviour patterns as obliging, and in this respect acknowledge a higher authority. But what they have in common with each other already ends here. In trade things are torn out from their connection in which they stand in traditional Economies. So things lose their intrinsic value and become *goods*. In extreme cases a person becomes a slave.

On the other hand, trade breaks also closed Economies and opened them to other communities. Thus goods from other societies may stimulate; however, most do not harmonise with the traditional forms of own culture. They complement them at best. If, for example, pieces of art from different cultures stand together in a space, they are not able to unfold themselves fully and lose their stamping strength on the people. People are forced thereby to strengthen their individuality.

Indeed, trade thus promoted the communication between communities and people, with a weakening of the mental content. One compares Greek art in old Rome or even classicistic in today's Europe to the original Greek culture and the meaning of the art of life at that time. These products have mostly only an aesthetic value today.

As with rulers, traders do not even produce, but at best have goods produced by others. Ordinarily they buy and sell only goods which quite exist. Accordingly they have a lord's consciousness comparable to a ruler.

If a person is completely integrated in an original *Oikos*, he repeatedly only produces what he has inherited from his ancestors. One looks, for example, at the production of traditional pieces of Chinese or Vietnamese furniture. The apprentices only learn to carve the figures perfectly and insert mother-of-pearl inlays in the traditional way. The most creativity that appeared was when they varied the traditional forms. Thus the same products were produced for millennia in their basic style.

To be able to really develop something creatively new, and this is already the case in limited measure if one varies traditional forms, the artist or creator must win distance to his present forms and materials, dissolve them reflectively and create something new out of nothing from the power thereby won.

This became possible in Europe when the practical Jewish / Christian working morale oriented to products connecting itself with the theoretical, abstracting from the phenomena of antique thinking mentality, which resulted in the natural scientific research. The more entireties are smashed in *entities*, the more the creation possibilities increase. With stones one can build houses and streets, with chemical molecules, however, the whole width of the chemical products. With atoms one can win not only immense energy but even make gold from it if one would want to do so. The world is transformed by scientific and technical creativity.

The capitalistic entrepreneur makes use of knowledge and inventions and invests in innovations, referring to a possible need of buyers, production plants and the necessary market development. In this respect an entrepreneur is more than just a trader. His ethical relationship to others is wider because new products and consumption possibilities are opened up to society.

According to the traditional moral rigor, housekeeping serves as model. This corresponds to original economy understanding which means becoming aware of natural behaviour patterns again. Hence, there is originally no saving as such and especially not as a virtue. Just like an animal only eats in accordance with its species and state-of-health, a person should also not save in the real sense of what he needs, but instead should only consume as much as he needs as correspondingly his status *befits* for him. It should only be saved for bad times and old age and to give an existence basis to descendants. At best the rise to a higher social class should thereby be allowed to the children. Of course, with a higher social class, the standard of living also increases. Who did not follow the rules of his social status, was looked at disapprovingly by his status comrades and was also not recognised by others.

Along with this house father's morality, the "heavy lot" of the entrepreneurs (who would have to renounce immediate consumption if they invest) is also described. So the purpose of enterprise action is mostly only seen as being able to consume more later.

However, both are crazy opinions. Wealth is practically never earned by manual labour and *knitting socks,* but rather by robbery and conquest and the possibility conditioned thereby to let work others for himself. This was valid for the aristocratic suppression of the farmers, and later also for the so-called *primary accumulation*, which in our days can be observed in the development of the employers in Russia. At best the starting capital was procured by inventions and trade, and was complemented later in the form of the shares and loan admission from those who were already rich.

Provided that an inventor or entrepreneur limits his consumption and spends all available means on his aims, he will of course save in this respect, but as a rule will not consume more later. For a real entrepreneur this is only a side effect. He is primarily interested in his work, in which he wants to be realised, and later in which he has his self-confidence. A traditional entrepreneur does therefore not behave differently, than a development aid worker, a social worker, an artist or a doctor. The purpose of their action is not primarily consumption, because then they would only be able to fulfil their duties insufficiently, although they had the task in mind. So they also work in favour of society and the environment.

The inclusion of others as constitutive for ethical action also appears to their employees in the behaviour of a traditional entrepreneur. Together they form an *oikos*-similar community in which employees and entrepreneurs and this can be valid even for groups – feel like they are members of a family. Thus, for example, early employees of the German company *Krupp* were called <Krupp officials>.

So intense was the identification with the business. The identification with the enterprise was also intensive in Japan. Therefore, when the globalised competition made it necessary, to hand people their notices, it was felt as taboo.

Entrepreneurs and employees also identified themselves with their products. The standard of their products was an expression of their efficiency, that is, bad products reflected poorly on their own self-esteem, as well as the fact that the sales prospects of the enterprise were thereby limited.

Enterprises produce for the market of course, and have to follow the principle of profit maximisation. However, this was understood as a lasting aim. In this respect much emphasis was placed on the fact that the enterprise could get over market adversities, that is it had to have an adequate company equity and be able to use its own real estate if possible, and also to secure loans, and it could make sense to aim not only a core competence like today, but to have different business segments, so that if difficulties appear in a certain market the enterprise can continue to exist through using the other products.

If one judges capitalistic management ethically, on one hand one must value commercial behaviour, that is, to what extent selfish action at the market also promotes the welfare as a whole and is production-oriented, but on the other hand, to what extent the action also encloses the employees. This is also true for investments. For investments in products, (for example, arrangements and real estate) and also research and development and marketing, result from savings which are for themselves looked at as a renunciation of immediate use of income to which correspond achievements offered at the market, but however, flow back again as demand within the business circle.

A modern economy understandably differs in varied manners from former households. By the new and richer variety of products as a result of the industrial revolution, of course by the time the estate-oriented *Oikos* was destroyed (which determined what a person could and could not do) and that could motivate a guild craftsman, for example to limit his production if he had earned enough for life or could not sell his goods at a reasonable price.

With the industrial revolution and the development of the free market economy the market participants felt less and less responsible to meet the immediate needs of society. Under an ethical life they rather understood to invest and to improve everybody's living conditions by economic growth.

Only he, who himself is supplied and has developed into an efficient individual, can perform something for his fellow men and even the world. In addition, according to the saying *„If the rose dresses up, it also decorates the garden."* in a liberal society everybody is obliged to unfold his possibilities and to earn the need necessary for it. For everything, what a person does for himself, he also does for the society. He, who constructs a nice house, a park or even a castle, also creates income and jobs for others; at the same time he enriches his town or his region. Thus today we still live culturally on the cultural monuments of the ruling of the past times. Also for lower classes, life is more interesting if they can admire kings and successful sportsmen and/or artists and others with a higher standard of living and they are stimulated by them, as if all people are monotonously the same.

In spite of all inequalities which there were also in former economies – a headman also had better living conditions than a simple family comrade – an economy must be in balance like an early *Oikos*. This means that every economic participant can only take so much from others as he gives, but also cannot give any more without taking. This is also not possible in a real economy, because only goods can be exchanged there.

Nevertheless, in a monetary economy in which money is inserted between the exchanges of goods, it can happen that somebody, who sells goods against money, does not spend the money, but keeps it as liquidity, as purchase *claim*. Then goods remain unsold. Vice versa the money supply can also increase and accordingly goods can be asked, for which not enough goods are offered with the result that a too high a demand either dissolves or leads to price inflation.

V. Maximisation of strategic and minimisation of economic-ethical behaviour in the Capital Market

In normal life it is generally believed that stimuli can immediately lead to activities before they even reach the consciousness. If these impulses are emitted from other people, it is called *body language*. But all phenomena have a body language, namely in this respect they work as they influence us *magically*, without us making them concretely deliberate to ourselves. The further we decrease in the history of the humanity, the more distinctive this magic becomes interwoven with the phenomena. This imagined concept being interwoven with the phenomena is called *instinct*.

However, the real manhood begins with the phenomena becoming conscious when we concretise them, that is, make them concepts. However, from objectifying the phenomena, we also end up giving them, certain contours, and separate them from other phenomena. The living connection with the phenomena is interrupted by the conceptualizing, and with it how phenomena reach beyond themselves is also abolished.

The first conceptually objectified things were imagined as mythical beings: mountains as giants, a pond as a mermaid, weather as an active God etc... In the course of becoming a self of men, which walks along with the ability to think and has consciously sensual realisation, the conceptually imagined phenomena lost, if you will, their *subject status*, but not yet their effect on us along with it. Thus nevertheless every appearance conceptually objectified, like a flower, a table, a bicycle, a father etc. has an emotional impact on us.

This emotional experience stops with the disappearance of the phenomena, whether the appearance itself passes, or whether one turns away from it. However, as a *concept* the experience continues, and it can always be visualised again regardless of the concrete appearance.

This led to the idea that the emotional experience is only *embodied* in the concrete fleeting phenomena and therefore does not purely exist as pure concept, but is *dirtied* by the material form. The philosophical interest thus developed from it about having the essence of experience in its cleanness, to abstract the essence from all phenomena, for example, as the *beauty*, the *true*, the *good*, the *absolute* and to enjoy it purely as an *idea* and to be absorbed into it. Philosophy, that is: thinking in the purest form was for the old Greeks, hence, oneness with the *absolute*, the *true* and *good*. The most general form of conceptual objects is the *being*. For, everything what is imagined and to which I refer, or it to me, is *being*.

The way gods, as *expressionless movers,* animate thinking the phenomena and lead their being and development, means a reasonable person steers his sensuous life according to the ideas of the good and true. In the course of the individuation of men, the gods dawned and the person either moved in the divine position or he did not feel the ideas any more as something outside him, but as his own being. He who controls the ideas has conceptual knowledge, and commands the concrete phenomena. For, knowledge is power and is enjoyed as that.

We also have a reflection for the conceptualisation of the phenomena in the economic development. Also there the concrete possibilities of utilisation of the goods became reduced on a general value, the *cash value*. Concrete goods have only a *life-backing up value*, as for example land, air, water, warmth of the sun, or a *value in use*, i.e. all goods which the person uses, or an *aesthetic* value. If one wants to make goods comparable with each other, one must reduce them on a general value. This is *money* in the economy. All goods can be converted into all the others, with regards to their cash value.

In the economy, money has the same function as the ideas which only embody themselves in the phenomena and which control phenomena. Thus money controls the tradable goods and achievements. So, one says: „*Money controls the world*“. He who has money also has shares in the power of the money, and monetary possession can be also enjoyed as a *power*.

To whom power is an end in itself, that is, who only aims for *power maximisation* and wants to enjoy power as that, is only interested in his own self. If somebody has a farm, a factory or is a jeweller, he still refers to concrete things. Who only refers to money or estimates everything what he owns only regarding its cash value, has lost the relation to real values. He also does not refer to other people any more, and instead distinguishes himself through his money rather than through them and, as far as they are dependent on his purchases or deliveries or on providing services to him, he also has power over them. To him, other people are not partners for whom he acts, but are to him rather only the means for the purpose to earn additional money. They are therefore no *ethical*, but only *strategic* partners.

Of course the reduction of values in use in *cash values* is a necessary passageway for rational distribution and a rational application of goods. After the passageway the goods also become consumer durables for people again. As long as money is only taken as a necessary medium to allow rational management between different economic subjects, it can be a moment of an ethical *economic* behaviour in the traditional sense. However, economic acts lose their ethical dimension if money becomes the end in itself and is maximised for the sake of itself.

Money has no intrinsic value. It is completely related to the realm of goods and has, actually, only the function to rationalise and to ease the exchange of goods what can be seen just as the fact that the money supply in each case must be adapted by monetary policy to the amount of goods in circulation. Money is also not productive as such. People have always felt that, and, hence an interest ban is also found in all religions and in Islam till this day.

This changes in Europe as money is invested; that is the credit grantors enable investments and want to participate via interest in the profit from the investments, but the interest is therefore only a kind of *dividend*.

Interestingly to thus take interest is also justified in today's Islam. Indeed, the granting of a credit must be in such a way that the interest can be interpreted as a profit sharing in accordance with Sharia, that is all yields are >>acceptable, which are based on trade or an investment in a certain product. Commercial financing, risk capital lending, renting, leasing and raw material trade is admitted. However, the most common investment form is the purchase of shares of private and public enterprises, because dividends are not regarded as interest because the stockholders own no binding right on it, therefore the capital by itself does not increase.<<[79]

As far as money is used for real investments, a saver would again refer to the real economy, and his action in this respect can also be justified ethically. It has to be judged differently if portions of income are saved without becoming purchases on the market once again.

Enterprisers are most related to the real economy that is to customers, suppliers, employees and products. Without intensely studying the market situation and taking it into account, and adapting the production methods and products to the market conditions, nothing can be sold nor produced, and consequently no profits will be made either.

The co-owners of a co-operative, of another personal society or an Ltd also mostly still have an emotional relation to the products which are produced and are sold in the enterprise in which they are involved. Also traditional stockholders are

---

[79] http://de.wikipedia.org/wiki/Zinsverbot#Zinsverbot_im_Islam.

often proud of the enterprises of which they hold shares, and have the feeling, to serve with their investment also the common welfare, even if the real motive is to earn profits from the investment. But these profits are expected primarily as a dividend as part of the running profit.

To such an extent however, economic acts lose their ethical dimension as the profit becomes an end in itself, and it does not matter whether the profit arises from the production of detergent, cars, armament or a brothel company.

The more a good's value remains stable, the more it is suited for longer-term speculations. Therefore gold and real estate are particularly appreciated. Specifically regarding gold one can observe the depreciation of the value in use in favour of the cash value. As gold was previously estimated as materialised sunlight and as divine and raised even more in value by artistic processing to jewellery and aesthetic objects, at the latest since the Spaniards melted the gold of the Inca, gold mainly is pressed in ingots and lies for good in dark safe deposits. What a crime!

Gold is not even stamped generally any more in coins, and then acts even as money. In 1971 the American Central Bank finally cancelled the ability to exchange dollars in gold. Why and for which purpose Central Banks own gold even today, it is not easy to understand, particularly as in respect of the fact that nobody expects a possible exchange in gold as the required currency for financial transactions.

Also properties and real estate are bought preferentially for speculation reasons. Trade with properties is favoured by the unequal property distribution which also monopolises the properties and real estate in the hands of few, and makes them as assets although extremely fungible. Who only holds real estate as stock, will speculatively sell properties and buy others in a quick and easy manner – unlike a real estate owner who uses his house himself.

With real capital market partners, stockbrokers and speculators it is not at all primarily about dividend which is earned from the real economy, but rather the changes of the prices of assets which result as profits. The price of a share arises from the comparison of the dividends to be expected with the current level of interest rates. Thereby everybody can win if the general level rises: if, however, it falls, everybody also loses. But, altogether there remains a zero sum game whereby the profits of the winners are compensated by the losses of the losers. Mainly the savings of smaller more traditionally long-term investors are expropriated within the losers. Accordingly the action of raw material, real estate and currency speculators also has no ethical value either.

As far as capital market transactions are zero sum plays, they are already said to be ethically classified as *games*. A game is a social communication to which everybody introduces himself as an equal partner and must become active under the rules of the game. A game is a whole. It differs from a traditional *economy* by the fact that partners with different functions, e.g. teacher, joiner, consumer etc., do not refer one to another as so, but rather in principle everybody is the same. In the purest form a game also knows no beginning and no end. One looks at the games of dogs and children, or the easy ball game which only depends on catching and throwing back the ball. Then the sense of the play is only the joy in the rhythm of the ball flying through the air.

A play is ideally an end in itself and it does not pursue any special aims either from itself or from the interests of the players. The players completely become elements of the game. Therefore Hans-Georg Gadamer defines a play in such a way that not the player, but the game plays.[80] It is certainly better that everybody is himself, his partners and the play as a whole, as well as with the ritual Zen-archery the archer is himself, the arrow, the shot and the aim. A play is therefore often used as a picture of entire harmony because it is perfect and does not refer to anything else. A person would be perfect therefore if his different attitudes and activities are only variations of a quiescent entirety.

The ideal of a play is spoiled by being turned into a lottery insofar as the profit motive, and the image of possible success dirties the plays. The importance of the profit in the play affects how strong this pollution is. The unity of the play remains extensively upheld if the profit motive is as it were only *the salt in the soup*, the participants have primarily their joy in the play and profit therefore is more or less secondary.

However, with the lottery this is only the case if the existence of a player is not endangered by a loss. For, a loss which ruins a play partner economically and thus also humanely would have to also ethically meet those people who have unburdened the money from him. Thus a play would lose its character as a play. The higher a possible profit and a loss can be accordingly, the wealthier a player must be.

In general capital market partners do not invest income which they have *saved from the mouth*, but rather excess capital after their daily needs. Otherwise, it would be irresponsible to speculate on the stock exchange.

Though speculations on the stock exchange are to be classified at best as plays, they differ however from real plays in the fact

1. that they are referred finally to the real economy and drag into play the real-economic processes of the production and exchange of goods to promote the whole welfare. This is unproblematic, as long as the stock exchange serves only for the procurement of capital for investments and is not abused as a playing field.
2. that as a lottery one can win and lose, even if it concerns only a zero sum play where profits and losses are compensated among the players. Nevertheless, these plays can have effects on the real economy which can be positive if by rising share prices the suitable enterprises can procure simpler and cheaper capital. Nevertheless, the negative effects outbalance it. In particular in the age of the *Shareholder Values* the enterprises are

[80] see Hans-Georg Gadamer, Hermeneutik II, P. 128ff.

forced to make profit at short notice. Beyond that, takeovers of enterprises are financed and the enterprises are gutted[81]; the enterprises can thus be endangered in the longer term in their existence. Accordingly it is speculated in raw materials and currencies by which the real economy can be considerably damaged.

3. that speculation bubbles are promoted by the investment pressure on the capital market by excessive savings means which finally end in real-economic disasters. Though the speculators lose more money than other social classes during crisis periods, they can get over it mostly, at least if they have kept to the rule to adjust the risks to their free capital means. Then only the small savers suffer.

If one includes these aspects in the assessment, capital market speculations are only strategic actions, even if in a very sophisticated form. They cannot be accepted therefore as an *ethical* action and if they damage the real economy, they are despicable even morally. Only the observance of the rules of the game under the capital market participants is ethical. This only corresponds as morality, however, as a *crook's morality*.

VI. Economic-ethical necessity to overcome selfish economic behaviour in favour of an identification with the common welfare

In a working and balanced economy, only so much may be produced as is used. An economic balance does not mean that everybody has to do the same or consume and produce the same quantity of goods. On the contrary, the more differentiated the people are, the richer the economy and those who do more end up requiring more. Nevertheless, it is necessary that everybody only takes as much as he gives, unless his abilities are limited or not at all efficient and he must be supplied by the others.

There are differences in the standard of living of the members of an economy, yet everyone can take only as much as he needs to live his own life. That was not the case in a prior economy. Goods were only acquired to the extent that one could use them.

Castles, riding horses, costly carriages and valuable jewellery could also belong to the so called claimed need. A limit could be seen at most in the fact that somebody wanted to have, for example, more castles and riding horses than he could inhabit or use. This could have been felt ethically as indecent. Also the pressure on subordinates can be felt as not appropriate to excessive consumption

---

[81] See: *Wie Unternehmenskultur zur Shareholder Value Mentalität degenerierte und Kapitalisten zu Heuschrecken wurden*, in: Unkonventionelle Betrachtungsweisen ... (I), p. 69ff.

and, therefore, the behaviour branded as unethical. Nevertheless, economically a real economy remains in the balance when as many goods are bought as are produced.

If somebody does not spend his savings but hoards them in a liquid form, insofar no wares are bought, then a national-economic imbalance arises. Therefore, goods and services, which are not purchased, will have a depressive impact on the market.

Hoards make no sense to liberal economic theorists, because hoarded money bears no interest. Hence the so-called *liquidity preference,* introduced by John Maynard Keynes, has only a negligible size in the contemporary liberal economic theory. It is treated at most as a transitional phenomenon, until the hordes are invested again.

Savings also do not lead to real-economic investments if they walk at the capital market and only boost prices of shares and other assets in the absence of new share appointments.

Contemporary economic politicians and economic theorists celebrate rising share prices as times of economic prosperity. However, this only applies to enterprises where shares rise in relation to others. The share prices of the enterprises of-ten increase as a result of rationalisation, which often means dismissal of employees. Thus it is reported about the business development in the USA in the first half-year in 2011: >>The groups have profited ... also from aggressive austerity measures as a result of the recession with which, ..., thousands of jobs were cut. Many have succeeded since that time in satisfying the demand increasing again without having to recruit new employees in large scale.<<[82]

Profit increases on account of employment mean a national-economic income relocation in favour of the capital owners which is reflected of course in rising share prices. For, as it is further said, >>if jobs are created, this often does not happen in the USA, but in low wage countries. Though this trend contributes to the stagnation of the US job market, it improves the profit and loss calculations of the enterprises, however, positively. <<[83]

It is to be doubted whether this is economically a sign of prosperity. Not enough new jobs are created, as can be seen in the rising unemployment and/or the transition in precarious working relations. For, as it is further said: >>Instead of recruiting new employees, many groups rather use rising profits and cash flows to improve their IT equipment. From this, the technology branch profited which realised an especially dynamic profit development. According to *Standard & Poor Equity Research* the operational results of the whole technology sector in the first half-year increased on average about approximate 29 %<<[84]. Because

[82] Facebook & Co.: *Der neue Hype im Internet*, in: Rendite Das Anlagemagazin der Börsenzeitung, v. 11. September 2011, p. 11.
[83] loc. cit.
[84] loc. cit.

their employment, wages and salaries might not have risen to the same extent, the development of the distribution of income in favour of the wealthy is continuing.

If the share price rises because investors do not find enough new shares, then we have share *inflation* because the demand of shares does not find enough new shares offered.

If the capital market would work according to the axioms of the capitalistic economic theorists, the rising exchange rates which are synonymous with lower payment of interest or dividend expectation would have to release additional share offers for real-economic investments. Then the share level would only rise at short notice, until a suitable capital demand absorbs the capital offer again.

Thus free-enterprise reasons cause rising share prices. Speculations are independent to these developments, although they can of course be a reaction to investment pressure. Speculations can drive the level of share prices up and down regardless of real-economic factors.

The national debts functioned as an outlet which has prevented that excessive savings caused a depression. The states have taken savings from their bonds buyers, in relation to how big their debt is, and have transferred excessive savings via state expenses to consumption once again, with the result that the sum of the worldwide national debts on the dollar has risen to 40 trillion and, because the money was spent, Government bonds are roving around the capital market without any intrinsic value.

Because it is relatively unrealistic that national debts could, at most, be paid back from future gross national product, the believers of the state papers also do not expect that due claims are erased from public revenue, but only that the states can raise new debts over and over again at the time of the maturity of debts. But in view of the gigantic piled up national debts, the believers are less and less willing to grant new loans, so that more and more states are now threatened by insolvency. Therefore, the danger of world-economic crises grows with the public indebtedness.

B. Necessary economic measures to overcome the global financial and economic crisis

I. The restriction and reduction of public indebtedness

At the moment the biggest economic problem is the worldwide high public indebtedness. States which can no longer repay due credits, because they are classified as less creditworthy, or no longer creditworthy, have to pay higher interest or not be permitted to get any more new loans.

If one considers the present practice of the public debt raising, it does not concern the *objective* ability to pay the debts back, but rather the evaluation of rating agencies. For if one would judge on the basis of objective criteria, no state is able to pay back its debts without destroying its economy and with it would also affect the world economy and bring about social riots. Interest and repayments are normally only paid from new indebtedness. That is possible as long as the believers are ready to finance due payments anew with new credits every time, thus the indebtedness could go on endlessly.

But with what means should interest on national debts or repayments be paid? If an entrepreneur takes out a loan to buy production plants, then if the investments are properly calculated he earns at least the interest and write-offs on the investment from them. A house builder pays interest and loan repayments on his house from the saved rent payments, which he would have had to pay if he had not built a house, and also from future savings. If someone wants a bigger acquisition and takes out a loan for it, then he has to distribute his expenses of interest and repayment over a longer period. Besides, as a general rule, appropriate collaterals must be given for bigger loans. What should a state offer as collateral for its loans because the raised loans will be spent for social transfer payments, public security, defence, education, road construction etc.? For most of the state expenditures, no counter value shall remain, which might have been used to repay debts.

To make national debts comparable with private debts, national debts should only be taken up for public investments. In respect to raised public debts, it is obviously supposed that yields are generated by public investments, as for example by toll fees on highways or by other public expenses, the GDP also increases, and with it the state revenues.

This expectation is justified up to a certain degree, but it does not however, explain the dimensions of the public indebtedness. Of course there are cases where public money is wasted over and over again.

Nevertheless, if one compares the needs of the private person, and in particular those of the upper property and income subscribers, with the public need of social expenses, education, infrastructures etc., the slogan fallen out of fashion in the meantime "*Private wealth and the public poverty*" is justified. Almost every non-profit area would actually need additional financing. One thinks, for example, only of the administration of justice - *How many years one must wait for the end of a process?* - public security, school system, promotion of basic research, families with many children, integration of foreigners etc. When you look to the state, expenses are not too high, but rather too low, whereas the upper income sub-scribers with excessive savings are playing at the capital market.

If the principle that "only investments should have be financed with public debts" would have been taken seriously, then the taxes for the public spending would have to have been raised. However, the higher income subscribers would have been subject to a tax hike, because lower income groups can hardly be additionally taxed at all. Instead, the taxes were lowered for top income sub-scribers. In the eighties, for example, in Germany the top rate of income tax, namely for private individuals and businesses, was 56%. And businesses still had to pay trade taxes on top of that. Moreover, property taxes and higher death taxes were raised [85]. Accordingly in the USA, the tax on capital profits was >>still at 40 per cent during the seventies, and the highest income tax sentence even at 70 per cent. Under George W. Bush they fell by 15 or 35 per cent.<<[86]

So the debts had to be raised accordingly in order to finance public spending. Simplistically that means that the higher income subscribers, who also have to pay most taxes, saved these taxes, and used it to buy Government stocks. For they might hardly have raised their consumption by the tax decrease; and for gainful investments there is also always enough capital at the market.

However, liberal theorists maintained over and over again that enterprisers would invest their savings. But this applies primarily for middle-class enterprisers. Because on the capital market more than the interest costs of borrowed capital can be earned, small and medium-sized companies also use the so-called *leverage effect*, that is to finance their investments with cheap loans and play with profits on the capital market.

As result we can therefore find out, that state expenditures are primarily paid by the higher income subscribers, either through higher taxes on profits or higher grants of credit, as long as one does not raise sales taxes instead.

Because the state bonds are not based on collaterals, under realistic aspects the owners of government stocks can generally not assume that due repayments are financed by additional income, but can only hope that they are financed over and over again by new loans. As believers of such, if they were no more willing to prolong debts because rating agencies advised against it and therefore the play was finished, then they themselves stopped the repayments.

---

[85] Though, partly this loss of tax revenue was compensated by higher sales taxes. However, these burden lower income subscribers more because lower income subscribers have a higher consumption rate than wealthy people.

[86] Thomas Schulz: *Die Ein-Prozent-Macht*, in: Der Spiegel Nr.43/24.10.11, P.76.

According to *presse.com* the global public debt in November, 2010 amounted to 40 trillion \$.[87] Because this money was used for state expenses, 'rubbish' assets are held accordingly worldwide by creditors in this regard. If it happens that single countries declared insolvencies, creditors would have to write off the debts as is normal with unrecoverable receivables of private debtors. Thus states would be relieved of old debts, and the capital market would be released from 'rubbish' assets. One already comes to this conclusion if one follows the generally approved principles of the market economy.

1. Improvement of public finances by depreciation of the public debts through inflation

As a way out from the dilemma of the excessive general state indebtedness, economists also discussed the depreciation through inflation, particularly as it is assumed that the economic activity is also stimulated by inflation because businesses invest more. For, when the general price level is rising, they can pay back their debts more easily. Accordingly, the public debts devalue themselves.

This proposal does not take into consideration that where there is a winner there are also losers.

However, these will not be the wealthy of today. The wealthy will have fled in the course of inflation in real values. The losers will be the lower income classes, whose financial assets are devalued and who possibly may have even sold things of real value due to rising prices in order to maintain their standard of living.

Besides, those who want to get rid of national debts through inflation seem to have no idea of how inflation takes place in the present *financialised* economy.
To that end

1. either the savings rate must sink which would mean that the wealthy people spend their money regardless in Europe, just as the super-rich in America, which is hardly to be expected, and in the USA the import profit would have to dry up so that the supply of products decreases and thereby the prices rise, or
2. we will have a *wage price spiral*. There are reasons for a *wage price spiral* with regards to the living conditions of the lower income classes worsening. A lack of skilled workers in Germany, owing to the demand of high-quality machines, could lead to cost inflation, indeed, only because production is shifted to cheaper labour countries but not as a result of rising costs.

87 http://diepresse.com/home/wirtschaft/international/600609/Weltweite-Staatsschulden-bald-40000000000000-Dollar

However, a rise in the money supply is absorbed by the capital market and does not get to the hands of consumers at all, therefore inflation is unlikely. Hence rather too low a consumption is currently complained about.

2. State bankruptcy or devaluation of the debts to stabilise the public finances

The usual ways to remove over-indebtedness are moratoria or bankruptcies. In both cases believers lose their demands to the extent of which debtors get rid of their liabilities. This would also have to be the normal expiry with an over-indebtedness of a state.

This conclusion also arises from a deeper understanding of the economic acts after which all income must be spent "real-economically" again, because otherwise the economical balance of supply and demand of goods is disturbed.

Therefore, if savers do not need income for either their own consumption or real economic investments, it is economically and morally correct that these profits are taxed away. If that is not done, the excessive savings will walk on the capital market, and capitalism changes into *casino capitalism*. Then one can only hope that the economically excessive savings, as far as they are not invested, are burnt at the capital market as *savings,* that is: in one way or another they flow back again into the real economy as consumption demand, for example, via income of finance service providers.

Instead of welcoming, however, that the states lose their debts and 'rubbish' assets disappear from the market in the course of a state bankruptcy, the only measures almost ever discussed are about how it can be avoided that creditors of the national debts suffer the realisation of losses by transferring the losses to the taxpayers.

Why is that so? Why are disasters expected as a result from state bankruptcies?

Certainly these fears are not totally foundless. All avoidance strategies to extend old debts, or to even pay them back, do not solve the problems. Therefore, though the depreciation of the debts is welcomed, what happens after a state bankruptcy must be realised. Let's look at the expected results of a state bankruptcy:

1. If states will not be helped to satisfy their believers, then the investors will lose more and more trust in Government stocks and also classify more and more other states as credit unworthy. This is an entitled expectation as the experience shows after the Greece crisis. Nevertheless, it must be doubted whether financial securities for the Greek national debts for preventing devaluation really excludes other degradations, and almost does not encourage other degradations; thereby the capacity of the community of states to take over the risks would not be overwhelmed.

2. The argument: "Insolvent states will not be able to receive loans at the capital market in the future", is to be doubted.
   Apart from the fact that the states should impose on themselves general debt braking, as a result of state bankruptcy, it could be fixed that only old debts will not be repaid any more. With it, the country becomes loan-worthy again for new debts, namely the more radically the debt is cut. As a matter of fact it would then be substantially more unproblematic to guarantee new debts by other countries, than to take over old debts and with it as it were *to throw good money after bad.*
   If a debt cut must be made, it must be done in such a radical way that a new beginning can be spoken about, and all new grants of credit can be put in the activation of the economy. Insufficient debt cuts were negotiated in autumn 2011, by which the debts of Greece should be reduced in 2020 (!) to 120 (!) per cent of the gross domestic product – but this will not be able to cause renewed trust.
3. Via foreign trade and necessary growing foreign help, the local economy will break down what would have an impact on the world economy.
   If a state (which is used to finance a part of his expenses by net loan admission) cannot pay its officials and employees any more, as well as its schools, police, the defence, infrastructure investments etc., then the economical demand of course collapses, with the result that the economy also must limit its production and services. Thus a depression spiral can develop.
   However, regarding the national debts, if the old debts are devalued, then new loans which will not be used for debt repayment, will be raised more easily and if not, it is then only justified that the community of states or in Europe the EFSM grant necessary *fresh money.*
4. Further it is feared that the banks, which hold the debentures of states, classed as less loan indebted, cannot afford the losses resulting from the depreciation of these debts and thus also become insolvent with unpredictable results for the economy, because the whole payment system and the granting of credits to enterprises would break down.
   But then many banks would already have collapsed. Bonds have already lost value due to the menacing downgrading, and accordingly losses have already been written off in the banks. As a matter of fact, the banks should already most likely foresee an expected devaluation of Government stocks, and it is then to be expected that they have already sold them on a large scale. If they have not sold or even purchased these stocks cheaply, they would earn not only from the payment of higher interest because of the price decline, but also realise huge profits if the bonds are taken back at the nominal value with the help of the community of states, or at just a higher value than when they were bought by the states.
   At the end of October 2011 while the European states were still discussing to what extent the planned *European rescue screen* must also support

banks, Josef Ackermann, the then Chairman of the Board of the German Bank announced: >>„The German bank with regards to capital, liquidity and refinancing structure has never been in a better position than it is today". ... The bank has liquidity reserves of 180 billion euro. With a core capital rate of 10.1 per cent, the bank already fulfils the rate of nine per cent demanded from the middle of 2012. And a debt cut of 50 per cent for Greece does not hurt the bank in a practical manner, because these state loans are reported in the books with a value of only 46 per cent.<<[88]

Accordingly the French banks >>reacted calmly to possible decisions to the increase of the debt cut from 21 to 50 or 60 per cent. The French financial institutions, with which Greece has about 40 billion euro of debt, think that they can bear the demands without state support. Our banks are respectable and can raise their reserves through their own means", explained Fréderic Oudéa, boss of the bank Societé Générale and president of the French bank association FBF. If necessary, we will ask the stockholders and not the state, he said about the SocGen, and during the day of the summit seemed to be emphatically confident.<<[89]

In the event that banks still break down, the states must support the banks, but insofar then should become owner of the banks by buying the shares at the market value, or found the bank anew. With regards to the deposits of enterprises and individuals of insolvent banks, the savings of small investors are guaranteed to a greater extent by Deposit Guarantee Funds and equity participations should be offered to enterprises by height of the devalued deposits which could be paid back later on from profits of the enterprises. Thus the effects on the economy should be smoothed out. The banks should be resold to investors as soon as possible.

The fact is clear that the described measures are not unproblematic. But, as long as the states have such high debts and 'rubbish" assets are roving around at the capital market as corresponding to the national debts, the world-economic problems are pre-programmed over and over again by devaluations of the national debts of single countries.

A state bankruptcy was demonstrated in the case of Argentina about which Lucas Zeise reports: >>The most spectacular state bankruptcy in our day happened in Argentina in 2001/2002. With the blessing of Washington and the IWF the country had chained its currency to the dollar. That made it easy to take up debts. The Government and the banks only had to pay a little more interest for their financial assets than the US-American state. The connection of the peso to the dollar also had real-economic effects: Though the inflation decreased, the Argentine industry and agriculture still lost competitiveness. Foreign goods

---

[88] Rolf Obertreis: *„Nie besser aufgestellt"*, in: Der Tagesspiegel, Nr. 21137 v. 26.10.2011, p. 16.

[89] Rolf Obertreis, Elisa Simantke: *Ein harter Schnitt*, in: Der Tagesspiegel, Nr. 21138 v. 27.10.2011, p. 2.

overwhelmed the Argentine market, while Argentina lost its sales prospects in neighbouring countries like Brazil and Uruguay, where currencies sank compared with the dollar and peso. A deep economic crisis followed, with fast rising unemployment. The external and internal indebtedness of the state multiplied. Firstly, the Government stopped the internal debt service and then the external debt service too.

The crisis following afterwards was even harder for the Argentines. From one day to the next the import of goods stopped. Also the production further decreased because the enterprises that did not have any loans could not buy any more raw and intermediary products. The peso was drastically depreciated. The old Government was swept away. The domestic creditors came away empty-handed. Foreign buyers of Argentine bonds nominated in dollar, in Deutsche Mark or even then (then classed as young) Euro, existing as an investment currency since 1999, got paid out in 2005 for about 30% of the nominal value of their financial securities. After the extremely deep economic crisis in the first half-year in 2002, Argentina recovered astonishingly fast namely completely without any loan from the outside. The depreciated currency made the production of goods competitive again on the home market. In other words, the real wages dramatically decreased. Instead of foreign capitalists, Argentine capital refugees invested. Before the crisis they had transferred their money abroad, but now fetched it back into the country where they found dirt cheap investment possibilities<<[90]

For the removal of the present over-indebtedness of Greece, the right way would also have been:

1. extensive devaluation of all present debts. Small investors who hold Government stocks for the provision for old age or pension funds should be excluded or treated better.
2. issue of new debentures, as far as they are necessary to the stabilisation of the economy and the society of Greece. The European Central Bank and the International Monetary Fund should agree to grant or guarantee these means if Greece undertakes reforms which exclude or limit further indebtedness. But these credits should not be granted for Greece to pay back old debts, but only as so-called *fresh money* for a new beginning.

We can be sure that enough investors are ready to buy new Greece bonds after such a moratorium, because no devaluation threatens for them for the foreseeable future. Then, like Argentina, Greek capital refugees would also return again to Greece.

Of course, in any case, an economic recovery of Greece is only conceivable if the economic mismanagement is also removed. Thus Greece did not efficiently collect due taxes, and afforded an ineffective and excessive bureaucracy and a chronically passive balance of trade.

---

[90] Lukas Zeise: *Geld der vertrackte Kern des Kapitalismus*, P. 172.

Important economic indicators of the Greek economy

	2006	2007	2008	2009
GDP growth rate	4.5%	4.5%	2%	1.9%
Inflation: Annual average	3.2%	2.9%	4.2%	1.2%
Inflation: Proportional change from December to December	2.9%	3.9%	2.0%	2.6%
Productivity (EU-27=100)**	99.7	99.8	102.2	103.8
Unemployment rate	8.9%	8.3%	7.6%	9.4%
Public investments (% of GDP)	3%	2.9%	2.8%	2.9%
Exports (Goods – current prices)	20.5*	21.4*	22.8*	19.2*
Imports (Goods – current prices)	56.4*	61.4*	62.5*	52.5*

*Billion € ** Source: Eurostat

Source: Greek Statistical Office ELSTAT, 2010

Indeed, it would certainly be easier for Greece to lower its price level in general and to increase its competitiveness if it would return to the drachma (depreciated in relation to the euro).

The insight that a Greece moratorium would have been the right way seems to become more and more common opinion, particularly as everybody knows that Greece will never be able to pay back the accumulated debts. It is also to be seen that the next insolvency will come.

Why did this way not become gone?

It was feared that

1. the extensive Greek state loans which were held by European banks will cause high losses by the devaluation, and the states must carry out a new bank rescue.
2. if one did not help Greece that other European countries, such as Ireland, Portugal (and possibly Spain and Italy afterwards) would have been brought to their knees by the speculation, and thereby the danger of European banks and their rescue would have increased.
3. that by these rescue operations of the remaining European states also lose their creditworthiness.
4. that the euro will lose value as a European currency.

To meet the international speculation the European states decided to establish a so-called rescue screen of 750,000,000,000 € which was increased then even further and extended by a so called leverage effect with raised loans up to the height of trillion €. However, can the problems stemming from the increased debt of European states be mastered in such a way? Certainly not without running into problems.

The problems are only alleviated if the indebtedness is diminished and, to this end, there only remains the moratorium of insolvent states from the possibilities discussed to date. One must manage the impacts on the banks. But debt relief can-not be carried out unless somebody loses their claim.

If one does not want to go this way to prevent the risk of gradations of the creditworthiness of states and state bankruptcies, then measures would have to be taken toward the dismantling of international debt.

It is demanded that all states should adopt a *debt brake*, such as Germany did, as a measure to restrict public indebtedness. Of course the debt quantity will not thereby be reduced. Because, however, a steady economic growth is assumed, the debt rate would become lower and lower in proportion to the gross domestic product. In addition, the states which are already classified as insolvent should also pay back debts. What do the states have to do?

They must reduce their state expenses and/or raise their revenues.

Let's check the different measures!

3. Restriction of state expenses in order to decrease indebtedness and repay debts

During a *general debt brake* if the state expenses are reduced by the total of the present state expenses which are financed with net new debt, worldwide demand will decrease to the same extent. The net new indebtedness only amounted to 801866 million € in 2009 for the 27 European countries; and this is immediately 6.8% of the gross domestic product[91] of these countries. No more Government stocks could be bought in the event of a debt brake to that extent. The investors would have to search other investment forms. For investors of European state loans, this would mean that they would have to consume or invest 6.8% more of the European gross domestic product.

Because the real economy does not offer enough lucrative investment possibilities, the savings with which Government stocks are usually bought will also participate in speculations in shares, currency, raw material and other commodities. And if they do not become real economic expenses via the capital market, for example via the income of the finance service providers and the realisation of speculative profits by other capital market players for consumption purposes, then they can instigate a depression.

[91] http://epp.eurostat.ec.europa.eu/cache/ITY_PUBLIC/2-22042010-BP/DE/2-22042010 BPDE.PDF

Since the worldwide economic crisis of 1929 the economists know, that public expenses restrictions can increase crises and endanger both their own and the world economy. Nevertheless, all countries whose creditworthiness is downgraded, for example Greece, Ireland, Portugal and Italy, will be forced to drastically reduce the state expenses.

The effects of these cutbacks on the economy are accordingly negative. So the Greek Investment Agency writes: >>The admission of Greece in the support mechanism of EU/ IWF with the restrictive economic measures, which were taken for the purpose of budgetary consolidation, have also negatively influenced the GDP development in 2010 a year in which the economy will shrink by approximately 2.5% to 4%. <<[92] >>In 2011 in Greece the real GDP declined about 6.9 % compared with the previous year.<<[93]

It would make much more sense to demand higher taxes of those, who are so rich that they have a high saving rate anyway. In the order of the rank of unequal development regarding the income distribution between poor and wealthy citizens Greece ranks already relatively high in 46th place. The graduation with which the inequality is measured is the so-called GINI index[94]. It amounts to 35.4%[95] in

---

[92] Invest in Greece Agency, Investitionsförderungsagentur Griechenlands, http://www.investingreece.gov.gr/

[93] http://de.statista.com/statistik/daten/studie/14538/umfrage/wachstum-desbruttoinlandsprodukts-in-griechenland/

[94] >>The Gini coefficient is usually defined mathematically based on the Lorenz curve, which plots the proportion of the total income of the population (y axis) that is cumulatively earned by the bottom x% of the population (see diagram). The line at 45 degrees thus represents perfect equality of incomes. The Gini coefficient can then be thought of as the ratio of the area that lies between the line of equality and the Lorenz curve (marked *A* in the diagram) over the total area under the line of equality (marked *A* and *B* in the diagram); i.e., $G = A / (A + B)$.

If all people have non-negative income (or wealth, as the case may be), the Gini coefficient can theoretically range from 0 to 1; it is sometimes expressed as a percentage ranging between 0 and 100. In practice, both extreme values are not quite reached. If negative values are possible (such as the negative wealth of people with debts), then the Gini coefficient could theoretically be more than 1. Normally the mean (or total) is assumed positive, which rules out a Gini coefficient less than zero.

A low Gini coefficient indicates a more equal distribution, with 0 corresponding to complete equality, while higher Gini coefficients indicate more unequal distribution, with 1 corresponding to complete inequality. When used as a measure of income inequality, the most unequal society (assuming no negative incomes) will be one in which a single person receives 100% of the total income and the remaining people receive none ($G = 1-1/N$); and the most equal society will be one in which every person receives the same income ($G = 0$).

An alternative approach would be to consider the Gini coefficient as half of the relative mean difference, which is a mathematical equivalence. The mean difference is the average absolute difference between two items selected randomly from a population, and the relative mean difference is the mean difference divided by the average, to normalise for scale..<< http://en.wikipedia.org/wiki/Gini_index#Calculation

Greece. In comparison with that, Denmark has the lowest rank (rank1) with 24.7%. In Germany (rank14) it amounts to 28.3%, in the United Kingdom (49) 36%, and in the USA (91) 46.6%.[96]

Furthermore in Greece there is such a high amount of corruption because taxes, that are due, are not collected in their entirety. *ARTEjournal* reported: >>Every Greek family pays 1700 Euros a year in bribes. They have no other choice, because it's the only way to ensure everyday life runs smoothly. 10 to 20 Euros are necessary for the doctor; for 300 Euros every Greek also certainly gets a driving license check. The corruption is deeply rooted and is one of the reasons for the widespread sullenness of the citizens against state and politics.<<[97] It is said that the black economy amounts to one quarter of the gross domestic product. *ARTE journal* reported: >>The Greeks have money, because the budget deficit is precisely so high because the Greeks evade taxes. According to estimates it stands at around 30 billion Euros.<<[98]

Others estimate the annual tax evasions at only 12 billion Euros[99]. But >>900,000 individuals owe the state the sum of 41 billion Euros.<<[100] Hence, if Greece would collect due taxes and deliveries, and dam the tax evasion, it would not have budget deficits.

Recently England and France also took take part in the nonsense of reducing state expenses to avoid debts. Of course, the debts should not be expanded further. But why do the states not try a budgetary renovation by raising the income instead of cutting the expenses?

4. Increase of public revenues to stabilise the public finances

4.1 Taxation of the economic activities to avoid further indebtedness

4.1.1 Sales Tax rise to avoid further indebtedness

According to experience, sales taxes can be raised the most easily. Nevertheless, sales tax disproportionately charges those, who have a high consumption rate; that is the lower income classes. But this can be avoided if the basic needs are only charged at a reduced tax rate, in Germany, for example, 7%.

---

95 In relation to other countries the distribution of income was already based on data from 1998. Nevertheless, the differences between poor and wealthy have still generally increased since then.

96 http://de.wikipedia.org/wiki/Liste_der_L%C3%A4nder_nach_Einkommensverteilung.

97 *Griechenland: Schmiergelder an der Tagesordnung*, in: ARTE Journal 10. 2.2010.

98 Griechenland: *Milliardenschwere Schattenwirtschaft* ARTE Journal 11. 2010

99 Albrecht Meier: *Versprochen gebrochen*, in: Der Tagesspiegel Nr. 21 120 9.10.2011, p. 5.

100 Albrecht Meier, loc. cit.

The sales tax still primarily meets the consumers. Though the tax is raised via businesses, but as a rule it is transferred by them on the prices and thus passed on the consumers.

In respect to the economic development, the sales tax is only neutral if the private demand decreases to the extent that the state starts spending money again. If the state uses the sales tax rise to finance public spending however, instead of raising debts, the overall economic demand decreases of course by the height of the reduced private expenditures, except in case where the sales tax charges those, who would otherwise save their money and buy state loans. However, this will only happen only in low magnitude. So generally by higher sales taxes, state borrowing and also economical demand will be reduced, thus having a dampening effect on the economy.

Of course it shouldn't be expected that private demand will decrease to the same extent purely owing to not too high a sales tax rise. For, then a certain part of the citizens will save less, so that the dampening effect on the economy will be slightly more.

Up to now, capital transactions are released from sales taxes; hence the inconsistencies of the present economic system. Here a source of additional public in-come can be opened for the reduction of the net state indebtedness. In the mean-time, this also seems to be generally recognised. But the introduction of the so-called Tobin tax is still difficult, because all states should introduce that tax simultaneously.

4.1.2 Income Tax rise to avoid further indebtedness

The rise of taxes on profits is a sensible means of generating more additional state income to avoid a net new indebtedness; but only so far as they meet income subscribers who do not limit their consumption because of high taxes

For that only higher income tax progression or, in addition, a so-called *tax on the rich* needs be introduced. Preferentially speculation profits and bonuses thus derived should be taxed away to a large extent. Only a small part of this income can be evaluated as an economic-ethically earned *labour* income. The biggest part is *game winnings* and, hence, should be charged with a *gaming tax* before the real income tax. According to experience, although the savings rate falls with the super-rich, it can fall again and even decrease to 0%, thus state expenses should rank before deluxe expenses of the super-rich. By the way, this profit can also only be partly taxed away.

With an income tax rise, it should of course also be avoided that such small and middle-size enterprises are affected too excessively, because, according to experience, they invest their savings again in their own company. But this can be avoided by a corresponding tax legislation.

Although higher taxes on profits for wealthy citizens are to be recommended particularly in developed industrial states, as opposed to sales tax and indirect tax rises to avoid public net indebtedness, Germany has gone the exact opposite way; it has lowered the taxes on profits and has raised the sales tax and consumption taxes.

So in Germany until 1989 the top rate of income tax was still 56%, and then it was reduced further and further down to 42% in 2005. According to the aims of the FDP it should sink even lower to 35%. Indeed, the losses of tax should be counter financed extensively by subsidies due to be cancelled, of which wealthy persons would also benefit preferentially.

The value added tax gradually rose instead from 12% in 1979 to 19% from 2007 on, for the basic need, however, only from 6% to 7%. The consumption taxes also rose. So, for example, the tax rate for mineral oil was raised by a total of 126 percent between 1987 and 1999. The weekly magazine *Der Spiegel* reported in 1999: >>With the increase of 126 percent within twelve years, 52 percentage points were gained up to 2003. With rises of six pfennigs each time, the tax on oil was raised four additional times, and rose by a total of 1.28 DM. The German Automobile Club ADAC calculated that in 2003 the state collected about 105 billion DM in taxes from drivers.<<[101]

Of course the rise of the tax on oil also intended to stimulate the citizens into energy saving mode. Thereby as far as the purchase of other goods decreased, this tax also had a dampening effect on demand.

The reasons to lower taxes on profits for the rich were also:

1. the belief of the market ideologists that rich men will invest all their tax savings and generate growth; over the course of business development this belief was seen to be more and more wrong.

   With lowering income tax the then US-President Ronald Reagan rang in the *financialisation* of America which then also became a model for the remaining countries, particularly as the market ideologists postulated that stagnation could be overcome by lowering tax. However, in reality, lowering the tax ran in parallel with an exceptionally high increase of American state expenses financed with debts resulting in additional demand coming on the market.
2. the international competition attracting wealthy people and company head-quarters from other countries, through lowering the tax. A spectacular example of it is Ireland with an enterprise tax rate of 12.5%. As everybody knows, the financial crisis has made Ireland nearly insolvent. Therefore, Ireland had to take up the so-called European rescue screen, but could refuse the demand of the remaining European states to approximate Ireland's company tax to the European standard.

[101] Spiegel Online 29.12.1999

The fear of driving rich men and enterprises out of the country owing to high taxes on profits is not totally unjustified of course. An international solidarity should exist, and pressure be exercised on tax havens and tax laws, and the international relations must be formed in such a way that location relocations are complicated or bring no advantages. This is of course the easier, the more is generally accepted that rich men should be charged more in order to finance public expenses.

4. 2 Taxation of existing stock values to avoid further indebtedness

Sales taxes, indirect taxes and taxes on profits have an immediate impact on economic activities. They have a bigger influence on them, than taxes on already existing assets. So in particular death taxes and wealth taxes should be raised to avoid new net public indebtedness.

4.2.1 Death Taxes to avoid further indebtedness

One reason for the huge difference in the distribution of income is the concentration of property from generation to generation, that is by inheritance. The starting terms of newborn children thereby also become more and more unequal. In a competitive society, the same starting terms belong to all individuals within the principles of a capitalistic economic system. Concerning education and the early education of children, this is also recognised in general. Today the political aim of all parties is to improve the starting terms for underprivileged children through day-care centers and special conveyor courses. However, concerning the property distribution, *feudal* principles of the *inheritance succession* are still valid and this "feudalism" is the cause for the increasing property concentration amongst only the few.

According to the principles of a competitive society the individual work should be recompensed. Who works more, should also earn more. In this respect liberals used to proclaim that the development of the economy depends on the so-called "top performers". Incomprehensible however is the fact that they call also the capital providers "top performers".

But what has inherited property got to do with individual achievement? Through their nursery and education, the children of wealthy citizens already have better start terms than children from poorer classes. Why should the children of wealthy people have their property as an additional source of income? Especially those born wealthy can grow soft and degenerate to playboys and therefore may not necessarily be more efficient, than offspring from lower classes. Therefore, from a social point of view, leaving a bequeath of a gigantic property is a nuisance.

Under ethical points of view only inheritances concerning personal family related objects, or objects to continue a tradition, are justified. That is: As far as it concerns the possession of castles or businesses, and an heir continues the tradition, the inheritance can be recognised, but only to a certain degree.

Capitalistic used property only needs to remain in this respect in the possession of heirs as it is necessary as equity for the continuation of the enterprise. In the case of inheritance all property exceeding that purpose, and reaching beyond generous exemption levels, should be taxed or be sold by the state in favour of the treasury.[102]

With such a death tax regulation, the height of the individual income would depend primarily on the individual efficiency as it corresponds to the mind of a competitive society. The recouping of big property would also reduce the so-called "generation problem"[103] because the state indebtedness would also decrease with every generation.

Against the principle of a competitive society the German tax politics have also lowered the death taxes, and have thus strengthened the unequal distribution of property and income.

4.2.2 Property Tax to avoid further indebtedness

According to the principles of German Basic Law, "*property obliges*", and higher property in particular should be taxed. Indeed, a property tax should only become due for so high a property that the competitiveness of enterprises is not endangered.

4.2.3 Balancing circulating Government stocks with the national debts through property delivery

As demonstrated the national debts originated owing to the fact that the state partially financed public expenses with debts instead of raising taxes. If the taxes would have been raised, it would have predominantly met the wealthy. However, the wealthy could then buy Government stocks with their saved tax expenses. As a result an uncontrollable national debt has accumulated in nearly all countries, which has made the states the match ball of speculative creditors. So it must be the most urgent aim to balance the Government stocks (worthless in the end with the national debts) and to redevelop not only the states, but also to drain the marshy ground for devastating speculative actions.

The indebtedness of the states can surpass 200 percent of the gross domestic product (Japan). That is: A state would have to pay huge amounts back to creditors, in the case of Japan more than 200 percent of the GDP,

---

[102] Details see: Petersen (2010) p. 406 ff.; see also: Financing of the pensions from Death Taxes, below p. 117.

[103] See: *Die gespaltene Generation*, in: Unkonventionelle ... (I), p. 65.

However, such a huge repayment is not possible purely through a reduction in state expenses because of the disastrous results for the economy and social peace. Repayment from additional public income would probably require decades. Till then the states would be burdened furthermore with interest, and highly indebted states would constantly have to fear gradation and negative market valuations of their bonds at the capital market. So it is desirable that the already insubstantial state loans are balanced as fast as possible with the national debts. For that purpose a property delivery to improve state indebtedness should be taken in consideration.

The property delivery is to be formed in such a way that it meets only those, whose need is not affected. To have property as an end in itself, should however not be accepted as a value to be considered.

If possible, the property delivery should only be raised once in order to minimise the irritations in economic life. The model for it could be the *countervailing duty* which was raised in Germany after the Second World War from wealthy men who had not suffered or only suffered a little in the war.

The right to clear away the property delivery to a certain degree from future profits, should be granted to those who are obligated to pay property deliveries. Indeed, the income tax and wealth tax should thereby not be shortened. Reasons for redemption can be enterprise interests in particular. That is no enterprise should be damaged by the property delivery. So enterprises should also be granted the possibility to resign company shares to the state to the height of the property delivery. The many-sided criteria to be considered with a property delivery cannot be discussed here in their entirety. But we should consider the tips mentioned

Just as in ancient Athens, Solon could only restore the social peace by the fact that he lifted the debt slavery by which the slave owners lost property[104], so in view of the present worldwide excessive indebtedness of the states I think a property delivery to be the most appropriate means to clear away the old burdens of public indebtedness. The delivery should only meet efficient property owners who might also be, by the way, the principal creditors of the state debts and in case of public insolvency would have to realise the lacking substance of the Government stocks held by them as losses anyway. A property delivery would also not charge the running economic events, or at the very least much less, like sales taxes or taxes on profits.

Therefore, it is clear that more and more voices declare a property delivery would be the best solution to get rid of the state's old debts. The *Initiative of Wealthy for a Property Delivery* was founded, even by the wealthy, for the

[104] See: *Eine Solonische Entschuldung der öffentlichen Hände*, in: Unkonventionelle … (I), p. 109ff.

penetration of this demand. The co-initiator of this action, Dieter Lehmkuhl, explained in a contribution in the German daily *Tagesspiegel* the need of a property delivery in a unique way.[105]

What would a property delivery mean, for example, in the case of Italy whose creditworthiness was often gradated by rating agencies? If we'd look only at the property of Italian real estate! Andrea Monorchio (>>during 13 years, until 2002 "Ragionere Generale dello Stato" and with it the supervisor of debts and fiscal sins among nine prime ministers<<) said: >>The Italian families own real estate in the value of 4832 billion Euros, of it only seven percent are charged with mortgages. Every family has one, two, three houses ... With about 20 percent of this wealth we could pay the 950 billion Euros which the Italian state owes beyond the Maastricht criteria for national debts.<<[106]

Paul Kreiner writes in addition: >>Berlusconi with his property of billions of Euro radically rejects an access to the rich – economists in the country say meanwhile, that with an effective property tax the actual indebtedness of 119 percent of the GDP would all of a sudden decrease to just 100 percent, and with it we would get rid of almost all worries.<<[107]

II. The removal of chronically active and passive imbalances of trade and services

Chronically passive and active balances of trade and services are yet another problem which provides for disturbances in the world economy. They entail that the countries with drastically passive trade balances get into debt more and more to the countries with active trade balances. At best citizens and enterprisers acquire real estate and enterprises in the chronically passive country and in extreme cases, control the economic life of this country. For by height of a trade balance deficit: currency, national debt notes, real estate, enterprise shares and other objects of value must be sold to the foreign countries as an equivalent.

To understand the difficulties how to come to worldwide well-balanced trade balances, we have first to critically discuss the principles of the world market.

The efficiency of an economy depends, as everybody knows, on an optimal division of labour. No one can live lonely and supply himself. Even if he would live as a sort of Robinson Crusoe on an island, he would be dependent on the tools and procedures which he has taken over from others. Besides, his standard of living would be exceptionally primitive. Of course it may be an ideal if a person can be active in many different ways. However, in the end, the general standard of living depends on specialisation and division of labour of the

[105] See below, p. 101ff.: Dieter Lehmkuhl: *Reichtum und Gerechtigkeit.*

[106] Alexander Smoltczyk: *Salto mortale*, in: Der Spiegel Nr. 42/17.10.11, p. 112.

[107] Paul Kreiner: *Italiens Problem*, in: Der Tagesspiegel Nr. 21138, v. 27.1.2011, p. 2

economic participants. Thus one becomes baker, the other doctor, locksmith etc. The more qualification a person has already for his occupation, the more efficiently he can work.

According to these principles the world economy should function in the same way. Every country should produce and also sell to other countries what it is able to do best of all. The doctrine of optimum international trade was developed by Adam Smith and others. That is quite understandable in respect of countries which dispose of certain raw materials or where climatically certain food prospers especially well or which are touristically attractive. However international trade only concerns one small part of the production of goods. All other products are produced and used in the respective national economy itself. That changes with the technical progress and the capital accumulation.

1. The change of the national economies by the technical progress and its influence on the foreign trade balances

1.1 The impact of technical progress on the developing countries and their foreign trade balances and necessary economic measures for the development of the countries

Typical countries with chronically passive trade balances are developing countries. They mostly offer agricultural products in competition to other developing countries, so that the prices are mostly low. Furthermore on account of advanced production methods in the industrial countries, the products from developing countries are not even internationally competitive even often with agricultural products and their home production is destroyed by cut-price imports from developed countries one thinks, for example, of the agricultural exports from the USA -. Even with textiles and everyday products, developing countries are often flooded with cut-price imports from threshold countries, like China.

On the other hand, the need also awakes with them in technical products, drugs and modern weapons, the latter to ward off infringements from neighbouring countries and rebels. In addition, the developing countries also want to develop themselves and import machines and investments. Therefore, they tend to have chronically passive trade balances

1.1.1 The deterioration of foreign trade balances of developing countries in trade with industrial countries, and necessary economic measures to develop the countries

The transference of the principle of the division of labour on economic relations between different countries assumes in the ideal case that all people are the same and, in view of natural resources and climate, only have their specific strengths in which they specialise and thus produce an optimum for the world.

By technical know-how, and the machines and equipment won from it, a new element comes to the international economic relations, because know-how and machines and equipment are applicable everywhere if they are not just used to excavate raw materials. Those who possess them often have a strategic advantage over others.

However by the education of technical abilities and more so through science and technical progress the people themselves also change. Besides, in many cases they become, with the help of for example modern farming, independent from the disadvantages of the geographic situation and can produce more and cheaper, than the other countries which should be rather more productive owing to their geography. This applies even more to such kinds of production which are not bound to certain locational circumstances. So at the world market, countries which still have traditional manufacturing methods, meet industrial countries which have already trained for centuries to hone their technical skills and then still strengthen these activities by the results of research and development. Therefore the industrial countries can produce often not only certain products cheaper, but also absolutely new products. The industrial countries thereby have a locational advantage, which developing countries can hardly ever catch up to.

Most serious is the situation for those developing countries, which have not already developed an advanced civilisation, like China and India. So there are, for example, African states with raw materials hotly popular by all worlds which are torn socially by family rules and live in social chaos. But even countries, which know to internationally market their raw materials in favour of their national economy, are often dependent on the industrial countries regarding the production and subsequent treatment. Still the home self-sufficiency is often destroyed in these countries by cut-price imports and also of agricultural products from the industrial countries.

Besides, rationalisation destroys traditional production. In particular at the beginning of an industrial development rationalisation advantages predominate compared with traditional production forms. Hence, natural location circumstances of an industrially subnormal country can be overcompensated by technical production possibilities in industrial countries. The result is that in developing countries man-power is thrown out of the economic process, the working class reservoir is raised and only very labour-intensive products can ever be delivered in industrial countries.

Because the main customers of industrial companies are again industrial companies and skilled workers are also trained in industrial companies, industries tend to fall in few locations. This already creates problems in the industrial countries, for example, between town and country, and also prevents the industrialisation of developing countries if only the market forces work. However, one should believe that cheap manpower attracts labour-intensive industrial companies. They are not able to do this, however, as long as the manpower is not qualified at all.

Moreover international commercial offices control the world market. A developing country therefore has hardly the possibility to control the market and to optimise production under national points of view. Therefore it is understandable that developing countries have chronically passive trade balances as a rule.

1.1.2 What can developing countries do to remove the chronically passive trade balances?

What can developing countries do to remove the chronically passive trade balances if we assume that the countries have at least a functioning state apparatus? If that is not the case, a functioning state organisation must be established first, and this can be accompanied by painful civil wars. We find examples of it in Africa, Afghanistan and the North African and Middle East countries just in transition.

To reach a least qualification, developing countries must insulate the market and force enterprisers from the industrial countries if they want to supply the market furthermore to also produce in those countries. This development began in the sixties. It was only reluctantly obeyed at first by enterprises from industrial countries. So one tried to do a minimum of engagement in developing countries and started with packaging streets, final assemblies and, for example, in the pharmaceutical industry with the so-called *application*, that is the pressing of the pills and their packaging.

In addition, countries like Malaysia have demanded that Malaysians are involved in the enterprises, which produce in Malaysia. In addition, countries with raw material reserves should try to get the subsequent treatment in the country if possible also. This will not be easy when the raw materials can be also delivered in sufficient measure from other countries. However, on the other hand, cooperation with natives was also aimed at by the foreign industrial companies because the industrial countries could not overlook circumstances in those countries of course.

In the course of these first engagements manpower already had to be trained. Only, after they were trained, it turned out more and more sensible to use them independently for labour-intensive production of goods for the industrial countries too. The free market would have brought no industrial development in the thres-hold countries of today. Know-how transfer and machines and education of manpower were forced by administrative measures.

Industrialisation in economically subnormal countries must begin with easy products because only manufacturing can train the manpower. First the textile and toys industry and then sub-systems assembly of components were particularly suited for it.

An economic policy, which wants to develop a national economy against the market forces, is referred to as *Mercantilism*. With mercantilist measures the economy was developed in nearly all industrial countries, like England, France, Germany and Japan. From it one can probably exclude, apart from the export support for agricultural products, the USA, which has also never hesitated to protect their national economy in the doubt against foreign competition. However, the American home market was always so big that up to now it could renounce strategically mercantilist politics.

Of course a mercantilist economic policy with manipulated exchange rates, import restrictions and capital market restrictions does not correspond to the ideal of a free market. Market forces can only internationally optimize the economic efficiency however, if equivalent countries are concerned. The market alone cannot manage the developing of industrially subnormal countries, as can be seen at the example of the developing countries, but also in the relation of conurbations to the remaining country in the industrial countries themselves.

To develop ones industry, one needs a big enough market. That generally does not exist in developing countries. So a sufficient export is a necessary condition for the industrial development of a country. To the same extent a developing country, however, cannot immediately buy goods from abroad again. It has for it still no buying power, and, besides, the danger persists that foreign imports destroy traditional production capacities faster than new modern production capacities can be built up. So industrializing countries always had an active balance of trade and pursued a mercantilist economic policy.

Today these are in particular the threshold countries which pursue successful mercantilist politics. The more successful, the greater the market is in which foreign producers want to enter. So the authoritative threshold countries are China, India, Russia and Brazil.

If a country has succeeded in getting job order production in the country, then it may not stop its economic activities. It must constantly raise the qualification of the manpower. For, job order production is always threatened by rationalisation, that will be concentrated more and more in more developed technological assembly lines which also need higher qualified staff. Besides, the danger insists that low wage manufacturing moves away to other countries with even lower wages. Thus we have to face the tendency that worldwide there will be less and less technologically developed mass production in fewer and fewer countries. One thinks of textiles, house devices, cameras, mobile phones and microchips. The more multi-skilled and technologically higher graded a country has developed, the more solid its economic structure is.

It is true that investments from abroad are generally welcome because they tend to promote the home industrial development. On the other hand foreigners, however, should not control the home economy. Therefore, for example, countries like Malaysia have required that Malaysians should be involved in foreign society foundations as partners and in the management. For, only if even enterprise know-how is imported, a complete dependence on foreign countries can be avoided. If natives are not involved enough in enterprises, besides, there remains the danger that the manufacturing is drawn off again and is shifted to another country.

This danger is lower if home enterprisers and home capital are involved, and it is the least amount of danger if the employees themselves are also share-holders. For if the economic efficiency of the production is endangered the employees will accept either lower wages or, work towards the fact that alternative production facilities are taken up and thus protect the jobs.

Because of the trend towards the mass manufacturing, it follows again that few countries, which could develop to manufacturing centers, cannot sell their products at the home market, but rather depend on export. Because they are mostly still weak in the remaining economic areas and do not want to open these areas to the competition from industrial countries, in such countries a chronically passive trade balance can turn into a chronically active trade balance. The most important threshold country at the moment with a chronically active trade balance is China.

1.2 The turn of a chronically passive into a chronically active foreign trade balance by a successful Mercantilist economic policy e.g. China, and the necessary measures to balance the trade balance

The chronically active trade balance of China is the result of a mercantilist economic policy. The products of the country are reduced in price by political manipulation of the exchange rate compared with other countries and accordingly, the price of goods from abroad are raised. In addition, production lines in the country are protected by duties and import restrictions so that they cannot be destroyed by foreign competition. If necessary the export of sensitive products which are important for the home industry is limited.

Additionally the capital import and capital export are controlled to prevent that home savings are invested not by the home, but abroad and imports and capital imports from abroad do not affect the home economic events.

As demonstrated an active export balance is the result of a concentration of highly efficient mass manufacturing which cannot be sold or at least not yet on the domestic market. These problems were also true for the earlier developing industrial states. Therefore one can also not blame China for its mercantilist economic policy.

However, in the meantime, the economy of China might become differentiated and has accumulated high foreign exchange reserves owing to many years of high export profits; hence it can divert the goods streams of its industry in the country more and more and favour imports. The latter in particular if it uses its foreign exchange reserves to buy modern machines and industrial plants. In this respect China should fulfil the demand for a sufficient revaluation of its currency com-pared with the US dollar and China already does it. This of course only happens in slow steps, so that the mass industry exporting to foreign countries can diversify.

1.3 The foreign trade balances of industrial countries by tendency becoming passive in the course of the industrialisation of developing countries

Ideally the creative process of new manufacturing and products would take place evenly in all countries of the world. However, in the end, nearly all innovations go out from the classical industrial countries because the innovation competence is based on centuries of old western mental development. Therefore, production in developing countries and threshold countries are duplicated above all, or production is evacuated from the industrial countries. As far as they are evacuated, they are of course absent in the industrial countries themselves, that is, if they are not substituted with other activities, they cause unemployment in the industrial countries.

It becomes less and less likely for innovations that they create enough new products and new jobs to replace relocation to cheap labour countries thanks to production; moreso because, according to experience, rationalisation innovations release more jobs than product innovations create with new goods, particularly as new products are mostly also very capital intensive. The buying power also stagnates in industrial countries because of the release of the workforce and resultingly no sales of additional products.

Threshold countries can reduce the distance to the industrial countries by mercantilist politics with controlled liberalisation of the goods streams to an extent, and build up a more diversified modern society, thus the industrial countries have a counter-rotating development, and tend towards *de-industrialisation*.

The *deindustrialisation* has grasped all industrial countries in different measures. As an example, let's take Great Britain and the USA on one side and Germany and Japan on the other.

It is true that the industrial revolution started in England. However, the Englishmen were by mentality primarily traders who have a more reserved relationship to their products than manufacturers.

England and America did not particularly defend themselves against the drift of the industrial companies. Rather, they propagated the transition to the *service society* as an economic progress. Besides, they argued in respect of the rapid development of their finance centers which needed finance service providers always up to more diversified assurances. Headquarters of companies are also favoured by international finance centers and attract further headquarters on their part.

The outsourcing of services from production companies was additionally pursued as a possible way to further rationalise production. Highly specified legal consulting and insurance enterprises, financial collection services and logistics enterprises right the way up to cleaning companies can work and dispose more rationally because they work for many customers, and have a better know-how and more experience than corresponding departments in an industrial company them-selves. Production units relieved by services also could be shifted more easily. The services remained in office centers, as far as they were not immediately related to the production units or carried out on Internet subordinated services (for example, call-centers).

Because profits and reimbursements are exceptionally high in headquarters and research and other service centers, in particular with finance service providers, and the need for material goods is limited, and services from consumption up to luxury also need to be better developed. Health service and care for the aged disproportionately increased due to medical progress and the aging of the population.

From apologists of the transition of the industry into a service society it was expected that released manpower would find new employment in services. Service companies were referred to as "resistant to rationalisation"[108].[109] However, the practical experience has shown that the service area can be endlessly rationalised by application of computers and robots. This entails that to such extent that on account of *deindustrialisation* and rationalisation, released workers do not find new regularly paid jobs again, the salary level sinks and the manpower must change in precarious employer-employee relationships.

As a reverse of the development of the threshold countries the unemployment therefore increases in the industrial countries and the wage level sinks disproportionately at the same time with rising incomes of the higher income subscribers, and the social peace is thereby endangered.

---

[108] Häußermann, Hartmut/Siebel, Walter 1995: *Dienstleistungsgesellschaften*, p. 24.

[109] More details of the theory of the necessary transfer to a service society and the expectations attached with it in: Petersen(2010), p.200ff.

1.4 Countries such as Germany and Japan relatively resistant against deindustrialisation

Germany was not really as concerned by deindustrialisation. The differing mentality of the Germans from the Anglo-Saxons is also responsible for that. For the Germans' self-worth increases less when concerning undifferentiated monetary increase, than with a respectable manufacturing of concrete products. Besides, research and development were already strongly promoted during emperor's times by the so-called Emperor-Wilhelm-Societies, today Max-Planck-Societies which covered nearly all scientific areas.[110]. Thus Germany soon became one of the most important industrial countries with a very high production standard which Germany could maintain to this day, and which brought Germany a chronically active balance of trade.

This development was also endangered through progressive relocation of production capacities to cheap labour countries. Nevertheless, this development was slowed down a little bit (partly politically encouraged) by dropping the wages in Germany, and in particular by the readiness of the employees to accept wage reductions in order to avoid the drift of the company to cheaper labour countries. However, the rising need of the threshold countries in high-quality machines and plants, which activates the trade balances at the same time, might be decisive for the relatively favourable employment in Germany.

>>In 2010 goods to the value of 951.9 billion Euros were exported from Germany, and goods to the value of 797.6 billion Euros were imported. In 2010 German exports were about 18.5% higher than in 2009 and the imports 20.0% higher than. In 2010 the foreign trade balance resulted in a profit of 154.3 billion Euros. In 2009 the balance in the foreign trade balance had amounted to +138,7 billion Euros. In 2010 the current account balance according to temporary calculations of the German Central Bank showed a profit of 129.9 billion Euros. In 2009 the German current account balance had a surplus of 119.9 billion Euros.<<[111] This development continued and in 2011 the German current account balance had a surplus of 148.1[112] and in 2012 169[113] billion Euros. In 2012 the surplus was 6.4 % of the German GNP and thus 0.4 %points higher than what is acceptable according to the European Commission in respect to international trade relations.[114]

---

[110] See: *Unkonventionelle ...II.*, P. 117f.

[111] Statistisches Bundesamt: *Deutscher Außenhandel 2010: export +18,5%; import +20,0%*

[112]http://www.handelsblatt.com/politik/konjunktur/nachrichten/zahlen-vom-statistischenbundesamt-deutscher-exportueberschuss-steigt/6663646.html.

[113]http://www.spiegel.de/wirtschaft/soziales/exportueberschuss-deutschland-verletzt-euwarngrenze-a-878787.html

[114] loc. cit..

The German export profits not only influence the foreign trade affairs of Germany, but also the remaining countries of the euro-zone which can export less because of the euro-exchange rate forced up by Germany, and which feel tempted to import more than would be the case if they still had their national currency. On the other hand, the weaker countries of the euro-zone slow down the revaluation of the euro and thereby strengthen again the German export in countries beyond the euro-zone.

However, the weaker countries also fall back towards Germany within the euro-zone because they can buy the German products cheaper, as if they had remained beyond the euro-zone, and Germany would have brought in the products cheaper from outside of the euro-zone, as from countries of the euro-zone itself.

So the reproach that Germany has contributed to the difficult economic situation in countries like Greece and has profited from it in respect of its foreign-trade is not past all reason. In the countries of the euro-zone Germany could deliver even cheaper because these countries were not concerned by rises of the euro-course. Thus Germany has not only a trade balance profit to countries beyond the euro-zone, but also to countries within the euro-zone itself.

With the given unequal distribution of income in favour of a few the consumption rates can be raised substantially in Germany, however, only if the wage level rises and therefore lower income classes can consume more. However the last but one Federal Government (under the chancellery of Gerhard Schröder) has changed the social laws in a manner that the wage level sank in Germany or at least stagnated, nevertheless. Through wage renunciation of employees in industrial companies, which were in danger of being shifted to cheap labour countries, the *deindustrialisation* could be braked in Germany quite differently than in the USA and Great Britain, and also contributed to the fact that the active trade balance became further chronic.

If Germany would loosen the social laws again, it could possibly increase the incomes earned up to a certain degree. However, at the same time the *de-industrialisation* could thereby be accelerated and increase the unemployment.

Germany, and this is also valid for Japan, has relatively good economic prosperity in comparison with other industrial countries not only because it has not lost production facilities to the same extent as the USA and Great Britain, but also because it has developed its products more innovatively. For, today in particular the threshold countries, like China, India, Brazil and Russia buy machines and arrangements.

In the medium term it is not to be expected for these exports to cease. In the foundation phase of the industrial countries at that time however, it will come over and over again at short notice to possibly very violent burglaries in threshold countries, and then unemployment in Germany and Japan will rise. One only needs to look at the menacing critical developments in China. Nevertheless, in the long term the danger insists that the threshold countries want to produce more and more highly qualified products themselves, and force German and Japanese manufacturers to produce these goods in their country.

Thus in the trend the base for machine exports and investment exports becomes smaller and the danger of unemployment in Germany and in Japan accordingly increases, unless Germans and Japanese can develop new products to the extent of losing production possibilities. For that purpose the main focus of the economic policy should be the infrastructural development of their own country, from the family politics up to research politics and third world aid.

Nevertheless, if Germany and Japan limit themselves to only supporting the top technology, there will not only be a splitting of the society between poor and wealthy, but also in highly qualified and precarious employer-employee relationships, growing social tensions and further rising social expenses. Because no country has only intelligent beasts and wealthy men who can live from the investments, and the market cannot close the gap to poor and less qualified workers, a sufficient minimum wage level must additionally be guaranteed and secured by flanking measures. The present politics to at least protect the standard of living by the rising social expenses, which are financed either from taxes or indebtedness, cannot substitute satisfying appropriately paid work.

2. The change of the national economies by capital accumulation and capital transactions, and their impact on the foreign trade balances

What the classical economic theory does not consider enough with its description of the international market is the influence of capital market streams on commercial relations. For if, for example, a country grants a loan to another, the debtor's currency will be bought and thus increases the exchange rate of the cur-rency of the debtor but if not to the extent of the credit then the goods will be bought from abroad. Then the exchange rate raises the price of the goods of the applicant for the credit, and reduces the export price of the creditor.

We have the same effect if foreigners buy Government stocks, shares, real estate etc. and thereby raise the demand for home currency and with it its exchange rate. If capital flows to a larger extent into the country, the exchange rate of the capital import country can thereby be forced up or its dropping be prevented. The virtually classical example of it is the USA.

2.1 The foreign trade balance becoming passive by capital imports e.g. the USA[115]

The most important country with chronically passive trade balances is the USA. The reasons for it are:

1. high state expenses, not least for the military and military help in connection with international engagements and the cold and hot wars. However, these expenditures are not alone responsible for the chronically passive trade balance of the USA that can be seen in countries like Japan and Germany, which have comparatively, or in the case of Japan even considerably higher, state debts although they are countries with chronically active trade balances. It might be decisively rather:
2. high capital import in the USA. By the demand for US dollars meant that the exchange rate of the dollar was so forced up so high that products of the United States became too expensive for foreign countries, and industrial goods could be imported by US citizens more cheaply.
   After the Second World War other states and in particular the industrial countries, gained strength again, such as Germany and Japan, were the first to become interested in getting US dollar reserves as an equivalent payment for deliveries, which then allowed them to make their own currency convertible again internationally.
   The big American market lured more and more foreign imports into the country, because, whoever partakes on the American market, has such a big turnover that they are able to completely make use of the advantages of mass manufacturing. Understandably, Germany and Japan, and later the threshold countries, wanted to export to the USA and to that end threshold countries, like in particular China, fixed its exchange rate in such a way that they could optimally export in the USA.
   That is why today the indebtedness of the USA is highest towards China and second-highest towards Japan. China holds, for example, more than 30% of the US-state loans. That explains why China was so irritated when the US dollar was degraded by the rating agency S&P because China feared a depreciation of its credits to the US.
   However, the capital of oil exporting countries from potentates of developing countries and also from less industrialised countries also preferred to invest in the USA because the USA is the mightiest country in the world and has the biggest economy. On one hand, the capital imports promoted the deindustrialisation of the USA, but on the other hand, however, its development into an international finance centre.
   Because finance service providers generate such high income that it

---

115 See: *Die wirtschaftliche Krankengeschichte der USA,* in: Unkonventionelle … II, p. 112ff.

makes no more sense to save further, the consumption rate of the superrich had risen to nearly 100 percent. The expenses of the superrich promoted the service sector in particular, from restaurants, leisure centers and health centers, up to other services, like guard services etc. which became cheaper and cheaper, the more industrial jobs were lost.

3. Through aggressive advertising lower income subscribers were also infected in the USA with the consumption drunkenness of the superrich. They consumed more than they earned and got into debt accordingly. The deficit trade balance of the USA thereby also increased.

From the beginning of the eighties >>a restrictive American monetary policy as well as the high budget deficit (approx. 3.5% of the BNP), linked with a raised state demand for loans, led to a rising level of interest rates in the USA which then attracted investors, and demand for the US dollar increased<<[116] and with it a reinforced revaluation of the US dollar.

>>With the rising dollar rate, imported products in the USA became cheaper, while the prices of American products went up abroad. The commercial deficit of the USA (which was still moderate in 1980 with 19.8 billion dollars) already amounted to 52.4 billion dollars in 1983 and increased till 1987 to 152.1 billion dollars. This twin deficit let the dollar rate rise up and up. Besides, the American Government got under the pressure of its own industry which demanded improved protection against foreign imports as well as more stability of the exchange rates.<<[117]

As a result the representatives of the G5 states (France, the Federal Republic of Germany, Japan, the USA and Great Britain) in the Plaza agreement, >>on the 22nd of September, 1985 in the Plaza hotel in New York decided to reach a devaluation of the US dollar compared with the yen and the German mark<< >>by controlled influencing of the international currency markets.<<[118]

>>During the next two years the dollar rate sank by about 50%, the yen and the German mark were revalued, and one succeeded in reducing the commercial deficit of the USA with Western Europe. However, a reduction of the commercial deficit with Japan was not reached, because on the one hand Japanese enterprises reacted to the dollar devaluation with price reductions. On the other hand the exchange rate tensions led to a recession in Japan, so that the imports sank there. This led to the fact that the balance of trade deficit with Japan still rose.[119]

---

[116] http://de.wikipedia.org/wiki/Plaza-Abkommen

[117] loc.cit.

[118] http://de.wikipedia.org/wiki/Plaza-Abkommen.

[119] http://www.uni-tuebingen.de/uni/wwa/download/gs/ChinaWkoFeb14.pdf.

After the two-year devaluation phase the governments of the G5 1987 were of the opinion that the exchange rates would have settled down at a realistic level and agreed in the Louvre agreement to use its best efforts to support the existing ex-change rates.<<[120]

The inflowing foreign capital promoted the removal of America as the world finance centre and stimulated the foundation of services of which the success motivated the American economic policy again to deregulate the business activity of the banks, and to lower taxes and deliveries.

We saw that no new jobs could be created in services as jobs were diminished by deindustrialisation and rationalisation. So America suffers more and more from growing unemployment and precarious employer employee relationships. Jan Hatzius, chief economist of Goldman Sachs, said during an interview: The un-employment in the USA already amounts to >>more than nine percent<<. If one includes the unemployed people which are not captured >>by the statistics at all, because they are no longer actively seeking either full or part time work<<, >>the unemployed person's rate is at more than 16 percent.<<[121]

Because the extremely capitalistic philosophy of the Americans hinders enough taxation of the richer and always growing richer, the state expenses were financed extensively through public debts and there did not remain enough funds for running infrastructure investments in the USA.

Apart from other active and passive trade balances the world economy is characterised by the contrast of the chronically passive trade balance of the USA and the chronically active trade balances of their believers, in particular: China, Japan and Germany.

2.1.1 How can the imbalance between the chronically passive trade balance of the USA and the chronically active trade balances of their believers: China, Japan and Germany, be equalised?

The drama of the trade balance deficits of the USA and their principal creditors becomes clear from the following figures. >>In 2010 the US imports of goods and services rose by 19.7 percent to 2.3 trillion dollars, the exports about 16.6 percent to 1.8 trillion dollars.<<[122] >>The principal reason for the imbalance is the substantial increase in imports from China: With 364.9 billion dollars they reached a record level, while the exportations in the People's Republic of China only amounted to about 91 billion dollars. In trade with the European Union, the USA also imported far more goods than they exported the deficit here amounted

---

[120] http://de.wikipedia.org/wiki/Plaza-Abkommen.

[121] Maris Hubschmid und Henrik Mortsiefer: *„Die Gefahr sieht kleiner aus"*, in: Der Tagesspiegel, Nr. 21142, 31.10.2011, p. 16.

[122] cte/Reuters: *US-Außenhandelsdefizit erreicht halbe Billion*, http://www.spiegel.de/wirtschaft/soziales/0,1518,745051,00.html

to nearly 80 billion dollars,<<[123] of it with Germany 34.3 billion dollars. In 2010 the American balance of trade deficit towards Japan amounted to 60.1 billion dollars.[124]

2010: U.S. trade in goods with

	Exports	**Imports**	**Balance**
China	**91,880.6**	**364,943.9**	**-273,063.2**
Europe	**285,596.2**	**381,811.8**	**-96,215.6**
of it: European Union	239,583.3	319,194.8	-79,611.5
of it: Germany	48,160.7	82,429.1	-34,268.4
Japan	**60,485.6**	**120,545.2**	**-60,059.6**

Source: U.S. Census Bureau: *Foreign Trade*

At the moment the American Government tries to animate the economy by economic stimulus programs and money creation. However both domestic and foreign goods are bought with additional state expenses. So the trade balance deficit can thereby still increase. The fact that the American Minister of Finance wants to motivate the remaining industrial countries to stimulate their economy, and with it the world economy, through programs of economic measures, is possibly also carried by the hope that more American products are also bought then, and with it a possible further deterioration of the American foreign trade balance is toned down.

If additional state expenses would be financed by raising the taxes of the wealthy, a general rise of the state expenses would make sense. Financing by additional public debts forbids itself because of the high debt level already everywhere. The present economic crisis is not an economic phenomenon, but rather of a structural nature. So it cannot be assumed that by so-called *fiscal injections* the world economy engine can be started and then go on by itself. Rather the USA will not be able to avoid a mercantilist economic policy which protects the American market if necessary with administrative measures against imports which prevent a reindustrialisation of America.

Also the dollar rate would have to be settled politically in such a way that the globalisation is not affected by exchange rate increases as a result of capital import; on the other hand, however, America can function further as a world finance centre.

From this enumeration of necessary measures, it becomes quite clear how hard they are to be realised, particularly as they contradict American attitudes and circumstances. So America expects China, Germany and Japan to diminish their active trade balances.

---

[123] loc. cit.

[124] See U.P. Census Bureau: *Foreign Trade*, http://www.censup.gov/foreign-trade/balance/c5880.html

These countries must diminish, as will still have to be discussed, in the interest of a world-economic market their trade balance profits. But that does not necessarily mean that the passive trade balance of the USA is also removed with it. For, even if China, Germany and Japan take measures to come to a well-balanced trade balance, is open whether the American trade balance deficit will be also removed.

If the US dollar remains freely convertible, at least at short notice a rise in the price of foreign goods would raise the foreign trade deficit possibly even further, because the products must be bought in America as long as they are not produced in America themselves for a higher price than from abroad.

If capital would flow furthermore in the USA, the exchange rate of the US dollar will probably not fall enough, so that imports would also flow further, if China would make the Yuan convertible. And the import from Germany and Japan is already steered not through administrative measures on the part of Germany and Japan, but additionally through capital transactions. In addition, China already follows the demand for a revaluation of its currency, of course only in small steps, to allow a reorientation of its export industry. But the USA also have to do their best to balance the American trade balance.

2.2 The activation of the foreign trade balance by capital exports e.g. Germany and Japan

2.2.1 The activation of the German foreign trade balance by capital exports and necessary measures to equalise the balance

Exports of machine equipment are not necessarily correlated with an active trade balance. If Germany shopped in the same extent like other countries from other countries, it would not need to have an active trade balance. Germany does not shop abroad enough because the consumption need is fed and the buying power (according to the income distribution in favour of only a few) decreases the consumption even moreso. For, higher income subscribers ordinarily save more. They invest their savings abroad if they do not see enough gainful investment possibilities at the home market, that is: they export capital. As a matter of fact, a *net* capital export causes a trade balance profit of the same amount.

Capital export is of course also possible with passive trade balance. So, for instance, potentates and other wealthy people invest their money abroad because they do not find enough lucrative investment possibilities in their own country. In case of passive trade balance, the capital export plus trade balance deficit is compensated by capital import in the form of development aid, purchase of Government stocks by foreigners and in other forms. That is, a *net* capital export is only possible with an active trade balance.

The United States of America are the most spectacular example of the fact that capital export is compensated by capital import. American enterprisers and investors also invest of course in other countries. The huge capital import to America however, still overcompensates this capital export in addition to the American trade balance deficits.

To those countries, which export capital, although they have a passive trade balance, also belong all countries, with high saving rates, and the saving rates only need to be high with the wealthy and high income subscribers who invest their savings abroad. A part of the capital import in developing countries often flows into the pockets of potentates and is again exported and insofar it is not of benefit for the population in general. Then by height of the trade balance deficit capital must additionally be imported.

Usually a country with an active trade balance, and correspondingly net capital export, is looked at as economically healthy and as a model. However, capital ex-port is not a sign for a prosperous enterprise in every respect, but rather only for an efficient export economy. Besides it is not considered whether the economic participants, who do not work for the export become impoverished, for example also because the export profit has also forced up the exchange rate so that foreign products come cheaper to the country than they can be produced by the home, or the wage level is so deeply pressed that home products can have no chances at the market and also not be exported, or the exports can be so cheap because the wage level is pressed. In particular it is not taken into consideration that foreign countries have a passive trade balance to the same extent as the countries with active trade balance have export profit, and thus get into debt.

If a country with a chronically active trade balance forms a trading partnership with industrially weaker countries within the euro-zone, like Germany, then the other countries in particular can suffer from the forced up high euro exchange rate by the so-called *export masters,* because the goods of the weaker countries are too expensive to be exported and also cannot compete with cheap imported goods. Then, in addition, they often get into debt to the countries of the economic zone itself with active foreign trade balances. In the euro zone we have a splitting between the efficient northern and weaker southern countries for this very reason.

In the present economic discussion it is expected that the weaker countries will lower their wages so far and animate their economy resulting in their trade balance deficit disappearing. But what would this mean for the euro zone and the remaining world?

A compensation of the deficit trade balances of the euro-zone's weaker countries would be possible if they would export more or import less goods and services, namely in respect of:

1. other countries of the euro zone and/or
2. countries beyond the euro zone.

For 1. With more deliveries in the stronger countries of the euro zone these countries would either:

a) produce accordingly less, because, if they compensate the additional imports by growth, the balances would not compensate themselves. This means reduction of the growth or even the gross national product with additional unemployment. The unemployment would be shifted from the weaker countries to the stronger countries. Or
b) the stronger countries would also expand their deliveries in the weaker countries accordingly. Then nothing would comparatively change in the relation between weaker and stronger countries. Or
c) accordingly, the stronger countries would shop less from the countries beyond the euro zone or deliver more in these countries. Then the trade balance profit of these countries would increase further, and with it the euro zone.

The surplus of the trade balance of the euro zone would altogether grow in this respect, if

For 2. The weaker countries would export more in countries beyond the euro zone and import less from them.

With a compensation of the deficit trade balances of the weaker euro countries, the world-economic problems of unbalanced trade balances of Europe versus countries beyond the euro zone would still increase if the compensation of the trade balances of the weaker countries would not be compensated in regard to the other euro zone countries.

The liberal market ideologists, who control the economic policy of today, cannot recognise these problems. For them, all economic activities must cause additional growth and thereby all imbalances will be resolved. However, such a big economic growth, which would bind all worldwide savings is inconceivable and unrealistic, particularly when about 10 percent of the income subscribers earn nearly all the income and the remaining 90 percent should buy the constantly growing products and services.

If the countries with deficit trade balances should really succeed in compensating their trade imbalances, the trade balances of the countries which were active before (or even chronically active, as with China, Germany and Japan) also be compensated with it. What would this mean for these countries? Depression and unemployment.

To the same extent as the present export profits, purchases would get smaller in these countries, and so less could be produced. Of course, the enterprisers would also suffer from this loss of production and accordingly make fewer profits. How-ever, they would try to shift their production to other countries. Vitally only the employees who lose their job would be met.

Countries with chronically active trade balances can only diminish the trade balance profits by raising the price of their goods. The increase of the minimum wages might be relatively without any problems. However, the real obstacle for a sufficient consumption rise, i.e. the unequal distribution of income in favour of a few who have a higher saving rate, would remain. What is to be done?

The only thing that remains is to raise the income in particular for those who have a lower consumption rate, and with this additional income not only avoid further public indebtedness, but also promote public investments, research, families, education, culture, security etc., that is in the needs of overall economic interest.

Such a rearrangement in favour of the general public is also justified because the consumption need of the upper income classes is covered extensively, and they use their money, as long as they do not find lucrative real-economic investments, for the purchase of state loans and also for capital market plays. With a higher tax burden of higher income subscribers the economic activity should not be affected, if possible. Therefore, the approaches outlined below should be observed with regards to this.

2.2.2 The activation of the trade balance by capital exports and the necessary measures to compensate the Japanese foreign trade balance

The economic problems of Japan are similar, if it diminishes the chronic surplus of its balance which has made Japan one of the biggest believers of the world.

The active balance on capital account of Japan is still strengthened by the fact that not only the upper income classes but also the lower income classes (on account of the Japanese cultural circumstances) have a relatively high savings rate and the saving rate increases even in times of emergency, than in comparable other countries. So in Japan it will also have to be an economic priority to further burden the upper income subscribers more for non-profit projects. The fact that the un-equal distribution of income and property distribution is a cause for the stagnant Japanese real economy (deviating from the Japanese export power) was already discussed at the end of the nineties when one thought about why Japan did not recover from the real estate crisis at the beginning of the nineties, referring to it as a lost decade. But that has not led to any political conclusions up to now.[125]

[125] See: *Die wirtschaftliche Krankengeschichte Japans*, in: Unkonventionelle … II, p. 122ff.

In relation to Germany (48.9% of the GDP)[126] Japan (with 15.2% of the GDP)[127] is less dependent on export. But, the companies, which work for the home market, do not work as advanced as, for example, the middle-class industry and agriculture in Germany. In Japan, this means that many more jobs get lost if the imports destroy home industry on account of too high yen exchange rates.[128]

In the present economic development is not only to be expected, but should also be promoted, that developing countries industrialise themselves as well and pursue research and development, but it should also be considered that there are high-quality engineers and skilled workers not only in the industrial countries. Less qualified people belong to the national economy of the industrial countries too and may not fall back further in their income development when compared with the incomes of the highly qualified, if the economy and society in the industrial countries should not end in chaos.

Because the foreign countries are not responsible for the economic and social balance in the industrial countries, the economic policy of the industrial countries must provide for themselves the fact that the wages and salaries of the masses of the employees do not fall back too much. The policy is only able to do this in the end by the fact that it supports, for example, the home agriculture, that minimum wages are implemented and that import duties for certain cheap products are raised. Of course, that is against the present free-enterprise doctrine. But a market economy can only develop optimally within a closed regular economic area. How-ever, this order ends on the borders of the closed economic area.

As a matter of fact, an economy develops for the better, the greater the economic area, division of labour and sales prospects are. Therefore, very big economic areas should be created. But they must be defeated by an order or a coordinated economic policy.

A multinational economic area is the European community. Within the European borders there is consequently also a common order and solidarity which provides, for example, that means flow from the richer regions for the development of the subnormal regions. At the same time Europe experiences how many economic problems appear if no common economic policy is pursued through the help of the overextension crises in Greece, Ireland and Portugal.

How much more difficult is it to pursue a world economic policy accepted by all countries? It would already be a success if, like the European Union, other extensive economic unions would be created, and this already happens. The stronger these economic areas are intertwined, however, with each other, the more the states must tune their economic policy on each other, and a common outside economic policy must be pursued. The foreign trade relations must be

---

[126] WKO Wirtschaftskammer Österreichs: *Export und Importquoten* Stand Mai 2011 (bei Deutschland inklusive innereuropäische Umsätze), Source: EUROSTAT, EU-Kommission, OECD, http://www.wko.at/statistik/eu/europa-exportquoten.pdf.
[127] loc. cit.
[128] See: *Die wirtschaftliche Krankengeschichte Japans*, in: Unkonventionelle ... II., P. 122ff.

adjusted, if necessary, because otherwise the internal economic balance is disturbed. It is clear as well that developing countries make international groups produce in the country or raise duties on certain goods, therefore industrial countries should have to be entitled through the use of foreign trade controls to prevent that unemployment originates from imports of plentiful cheap products.

2.3 Foreign currency speculations and their impact on the trade balances

Speculative changes are the most dangerous for the currency exchange rate. As well as shares prices falling and rising due to general appraisals of the economic development or the shares of a single enterprise changing from its published profit expectation, the value of a currency can thus also change, without appreciable purchases and sales of it. Only the general appraisal that a euro should not be worth no more 1.40 US dollars, but preferably only 1.36 US dollars would already cause the exchange rate to change. Besides it does not necessarily play a role in whether this exchange rate corresponds to the buying power parities between the countries which should determine the exchange of commodities.

Foreign currency speculations must also have no capital export or capital import to the basis. At the moment Swiss Francs, for example, are bought in particular because the Swiss Franc is looked at as an especially stable currency.

The purchase of Swiss Francs is economically an exchange of US dollar or euro to Swiss franc, that is: Switzerland exchanges its currency in other currencies, it gives their Swiss Franc and receives foreign currency of other countries in return.

If two trading partners mutually exchange debt obligations, let's say €100, the balance for both remains neutral. If, nevertheless, the offer of a currency is lower than the demand, its exchange rate rises. With the risen exchange rate, the prices of the export products of the country are also raised and its import products are reduced in price.

This development can only be hindered by the fact that, like in case of Switzerland, the exchange rate is fixed by the Swiss Central Bank to for example one Swiss Franc equals €1.20 and, for that purpose, the Swiss Central Bank unrestrictedly exchanges Swiss franc in other currencies at this exchange rate. If Switzerland does not thereby want the increase unconditioned by the money supply, then it must take administrative measures, and this would mean a restriction of its convertibility.

The smaller a country is, the more it is dependent on currency speculations. The countries which belong to a bigger currency union, as the countries of the euro zone, are less touched by currency speculations. In bigger currency rooms the real-economic buying power parities can assert themselves better. Therefore speculations against government stocks of single countries of a currency zone can have disastrous effects which, via the expected effects of a debt crisis, can also have an impact on the general economic development and this can influence the currency of the currency zone, but would not have a such a big effect as if the currency of a the single country would be a victim of the speculation.

These connections should be taken into account if a breakdown of the euro is immediately derived from the debt crises of euro zone countries, particularly when other important currencies, such as the US dollar, are also very speculation-threatened. Which currency should the speculators move to without big risk?

III. The renovation of the Capital Market

What is capital? Capital is a property right which is used to make money. If I have a golden ring, pictures and pieces of art of approved artists, an expensive engine yacht or similar things, these are not classed as capital. It's only if I use them or I take part in enterprises, put savings in a bank or buy a machine *to make profit*, that it is then classed as capital.

If I use real objects to make profit, we speak of *real capital.* Capital can be, however, even vested property rights. With vested property rights I am the owner. But others who work with the equivalent of the property rights – juridically speaking – are holders.

In the course of the business development the amount of invested property rights has constantly increased because enterprisers do not have enough own means for their investments and therefore borrow means from others. The market on which the property rights are traded is the capital market. The job of the capital market should be only the mediation of savings capital.

In the course of time and in particular in the current time, the capital market is less and less a mediator of capital to investors, but more a *playing field* for sold profit expectations. Besides, it can also concern bets on expected price movements. Then the substance value of enterprise and other arrangements are no longer of interest, but rather only the very short-term profit expectations and expected price variations.

This development was favoured by the centering of property and income in the hands of less and less wealthy people. With wide property dispersion the emotional connection of the property owners to their properties, houses and enterprises and also their financial participations is much greater than with multiple millionaires or even multi-billionaires. The latter call even more or less anonymous assets to their property.

Furthermore it is also hardly worthwhile for a small investor to pursue stock market transactions and stock exchange games and to enter, besides, ventures risks. To a rich speculator stock market plays can become a hobby, as long as he does not gamble away his life basis. The profit or loss can withdraw behind the charm of the play itself.

Wealthy people are also expelled to the capital market because they earn more than they need for their consumption and want to invest this money again very gainfully.

On the ground of more and more fungible property titles a more and more diversified financial service branch originated which earned with every transaction and invented new betting games too.

Lucrative real-economic investments could not keep pace any more with the growing savings capital to such an extent that the speculation rushed to new areas, such as raw materials, currencies and developed an increasing sturgeon potential for real-economic processes.

Government stocks were always a popular investment form which was estimated in particular by investors with a high security need. For, states were regarded as the best guarantors for investments resistant to value loss because they cannot go bankrupt in the opinion of the investors.

Besides, the fact was overlooked that state expenses are financed with public debts and they flow, actually, into the economical consumption, and therefore have no real-economic equivalent. Only a fraction of the state expenses are used for infrastructure investments. Only in respect of these infrastructure expenses one could argue that they also serve the economy and therefore generate higher taxes.

Nevertheless, such calculations hardly make sense and so they are not made. As far as infrastructure investments really increase state revenues and are not used for new duties again, that is, originate profits, taxes are mostly lowered and debts will only be erased with especially high national indebtedness.

Actually due public debts are financed by new debt admissions in each case and, as long as that functions, it is carried out even further. If single states then become insolvent, just the believers must renounce the repayment of their loans.

Because the public indebtedness has reached an inconceivable height, both worldwide, and also in particular in industrial countries, insolvency today threatens more and more countries by which then also other countries can be pulled in the whirlpool and the whole world economy is endangered. So the capital market must be redeveloped.

For that purpose the following economic and tax-political measures may be pursued:

1. Reduction of the investment pressure on the capital market
2. Discharge of the capital market of trade with state loans
3. Ban or licensing and taxation of betting games
4. Slow down of the capital market transactions by transaction taxes
5. Aggravation of the monetary procurement for capital market transactions

1. Reduction of the investment pressure on the Capital Market

The real job of the capital market is the mediation of savings to investors. The higher the savings are, the higher the *investment pressure* is. The amount of the savings is also dependent on the income distribution, that is the savings volume rises in line with the movement of the incomes in favour of the few wealthy people. To that extent the savings must be invested. Otherwise goods and services remain unsold and economic depressions result from that.

Real-economic investments are realised if they promise profit. Profits first increase with rationalisation investments, because earned incomes thereby becomes capital income, and secondly enlargement investments. Rationalisation investments can of course walk along with enlargement investments if the sales can be also extended to the extent of the realisation.

In threshold countries with real-economic investments, the production and the sales prospects rise, and the latter as well at the domestic market as, because of cheap labour costs, for goods to be exported. Accordingly these countries have astonishingly high growth rates. But the sales at the domestic market also limp behind the profits of the enterprisers, so that the capital walks on the international capital market, mainly in large scale in the world finance centers.

In the industrial countries the general standard of living is higher than in developing countries. Consequently it is saved in general more by the unequal distribution of income in favour of only a few. So the economy cannot grow in the industrial countries strongly, and as a result of that it binds fewer savings.[129]

The savings not used for real-economic investments are active at the capital market in speculations with shares, raw materials, currencies, gold, real estate etc. So far the economic policy and tax politics succeed in taxing away excessive savings and to spend it for charitable purposes they can thus contribute to the stabilisation of the capital market.

2. Discharge of the Capital Market from trade with State loans

State loans are also traded on the Capital Market, although the money raised is not used for profit orientated investments, but for consumption expenses.

State expenses are used for public need and/or necessary transfer payments, hence, would have to be financed from running income. In this respect, it can only be justified to pay state expenses with loans when a future profit it to be expected on account of given or raised tax rates, through which present finance gaps can be compensated. This principle also forms the basis of the anti-cyclical economic policy according to which the state should shop more in times of depression, that is when private purchases are economically not enough, and should pay back debts in boom times when private buy economically excessively.

[129] See: *Warum muss eine Wirtschaft wachsen?* In: *Unkonventionelle* ... I, p.27ff.

Nevertheless, the economic practice hardly followed this principle; the debts therefore rose on and on.[130] So, basically state expenses should not be financed, except in special situations, by public debts. This is why the anchorage of a general debt brake in the constitution of a country is right. If the state wants or is economically forced to spend more, it must shorten either other expenses - we saw which problems are connected with expenditure cuts from economic and social points of view -[131] or raise its income.

Besides, increases of taxes for growing state expenditures cause less savings supply on the capital market, and these means are available for public tasks if they meet above all those, who would only save instead of tax payments. So higher taxes help stabilise the economic situation.

Nevertheless, by additional taxes and deliveries from the actual gross national product only further net indebtedness should be avoided. Against it, old debts refer to state expenses of former economic periods. They should be paid back with taxes on assets (wealth taxes and death taxes) for reasons cited above so as not to damage the topical economic events. We come back to it.

Other possibilities for the reduction of the national debts arise from a reorganisation of the money market (look there!)

3. Ban or licensing and taxation of betting games

The capital market has to serve the economy and is not a casino. Consequently every form of speculative betting games should be forbidden.

Up to now European countries have only come to an agreement about a ban of so-called uncovered short sales that is the speculation on falling prices. A worldwide ban which hinders an elusiveness of such activities in other countries is still pending.

Hedging transactions should of course not be affected by the ban with which income and expenses are guaranteed for goods deliveries at a later time.

It should be considered that a lot of capital is burnt by speculative capital market transactions and so flows again into consumption. One thinks of the expenditures of finance service providers with a savings rate of close to 0%. If one wants therefore to impose no bans, however, capital market games should be treated as equal to other gambling (lotto etc.) and be charged with gaming taxes.

Although, no taxes result on lotto and winnings in casinos because they are already taxed away before, however, gaming taxes should be raised also differently from present speculation taxes, directly from the winnings and regardless of the income tax. That is: the remaining profit would be also be burdened by the normal income tax.

---

[130] See: *Unkonventionell* ... II, p.17.

[131] loc. cit., p.31ff.

Excessive savings are taxed away in this respect by a gaming tax and can serve to finance public duties. By height of the absorptions they are also no longer available for speculation plays.

4. The Slowdown of Capital Market Transactions by Transaction Taxes

Every day trillions of euro capital market transactions hunt around the globe. Klaus Stocker writes: >>The payments from commercial transactions, so imports and exports, are only responsible for approximately 1.3% (!) of the world-wide capital movements ([132]).<<[133]

It is not very understandable why every real-economic turnover is charged with sales taxes and also real estate purchases with real estate transfer taxes, yet speculative capital market transactions, are not.

Regardless of such a justice feeling the US-American economist James Tobin recommended >>in 1972 to dam the short-term speculation on currency fluctuations by a very low tax on all international foreign currency transactions. He hoped that with such a tax that the exchange rates of currencies would more strongly reflect the long-term real-economic phenomena than the short-term speculative expectations<<[134] Therefore such a tax is called *Tobin tax*.

According to his calculation if a tax results with every transaction, the investors will have to decide whether they restack immediately in other investment form or wait, until a clear trend stands out. The less fast investors restack, the less they also motivate others to similar actions, so that it does not need to come to high price fluctuations of securities at short notice any more.

Others saw in such a tax at the same time an additional possibility to finance developing countries.

The policy has long been against the Tobin tax. The policy only had, and still has, to face the growing turbulence at the capital market and the huge financial means, to renovate the banks, and has thus led to a change in thinking. >>At the beginning of 2005 the former president of France Jacque Chirac and Federal Chancellor Gerhard Schröder (SPD) declared themselves in favour of a Tobin tax. After a little while the Federal Chancellor of Austria Wolfgang Schüssel followed. The CSU still needed till 2010.

Then at the end of September 2011 EU-Commission President José Manuel Barroso suggested >>a financial transaction tax throughout Europe. Specifically he thinks of a tax at the rate of 0.1 percent on trade with shares and loans. By the sales and buying of derivatives should be cashed up 0.01 percent. He counts on

---

[132] Bank für internationalen Zahlungsausgleich (BIZ) Triennial Central Bank Survey of Foreign Research and Derivative Market Activity, Basel 2004 (2004 a) P. 1ff. ... and IMF Financial Statistic Yearbook 2003, pp. 81 ...

[133] Klaus Stocker: *Management internationaler Finanz und Währungsrisiken, p. 3.*

[134] http://de.wikipedia.org/wiki/Tobin-Steuer.

annual tax revenues of 55 billion euro, said Barroso ... before the EU parliament in Strasbourg. The transaction tax should come into force as from 1st of January, 2014 in all 27 EU countries, according to his proposal. The tax should not be valid, however, for private consumer purchases, possibly of assurances, mortgages or loans.<<[135]

As a counter-argument up to now it was always stated that a single state or also a state group cannot introduce such a tax because the speculators then make their way over to other countries. Nevertheless eleven European states have decided to go ahead with the introduction of this tax. The present considerations consider raising the tax for European citizens no matter where they carry out the transactions. In addition, evasive actions might not be possibly worthwhile because the taxes were only planned up to now with 0.1-1 percent. Nevertheless, the relatively low amount may be dealable for speculators. It may still be debatable whether this low rate can hold them so from short-term capital transactions which promise, nevertheless, mostly much higher profits or avoid losses. In this respect with such a tax it is still only in its beginning stages, so can still be developed.

IV. The renovation of the Money Market

The deregulations of the business activities of the banks are generally looked at as the cause of the financial and economic crisis and will still continue to do so. Thereby the possibility of the banks to create credits was steadily increased.

The volume of money in circulation is not only cash which flows from the central banks into the economy as equivalent of securities, gold and currencies of other countries bought by the central bank and then available for payments or also hoarded as money. You can also pay with a credit of a commercial bank which is transferred to another bank. Bank deposits can be created by the commercial banks by granting a credit. Because these deposits bank are created as a book process, one calls them "scriptural money".

How much scriptural money a bank can create, depends on the fact of how many payments are effected in cash and how many as bank credit transfers. The banks must only provide for the fact that the usual cash payment demanded by the customers is as high as cash payments received by the bank. With a functioning bank system this rule is valid for the bank system all together. To fulfil this condition single banks can borrow cash needed at short notice from others.[136]

[135] Mathias Richter: *Der Präsident der EU-Kommission schlägt eine EU-weite Finanztransaktionssteuer vor*, in: Märkische Allgemeine, 29.9.2011

[136] More details in: Petersen (2010a), P. 59ff.

If the trust of the banks to one another is shaken however (as it was the case after the last financial crisis), then the banks fear that partner banks can possibly become insolvent and not repay granted liquidity credits. So the interbank credits nearly finished with the result that banks could not any more trust to get needed liquidity and it thus restricted their money creation.

Accordingly cautiously the banks granted credits and thereby increased the economic crisis. Therefore the central banks had to pump more central bank money into the economy as a balance for diminishing scriptural money, so that the payments were not strangled.

To avoid bank failures, the policy does not count on the fact about whether the banks are always cautious enough with how much credits they grant, but instead gives rules to them, for example, how much equity they must have concerning which kind of granted credits.

Thereby the central banks found out that their maxim was no longer valid: that money increases always automatically cause inflation. For, also capital market transactions need liquidity for real-economic payments, which is many times higher than what is needed for real-economic payments.[137] The need of currency is accordingly high. Besides, the additional money did not flow any more into the hands of the consumers, but in the hands of the capital market players because of the deindustrialisation as a result of the globalisation and weakening of the trade unions. So it did not cause a rise of the purchases of real-economic goods any more.

Additionally it has to be taken into account that the banks earn much more with the mediation and consulting of effected capital market games, than with granting credits to enterprises or private persons. So a cutback of the money supply primarily meets the real economy.

A money supply restriction would primarily have to strangle the economy under these points of view. So outgoing from the USA the central banks saw less and less sense in adjusting the business activity of the banks. Therefore, the central banks ceased the limitations of the commercial banks to grant credits more and more. In addition, the central banks also raised the money supply if they had the feeling that the economy needed more liquidity. So the general money increase is not a cause of the economic crisis, but should prevent depressions of the real economy.

As long as the capital market itself does not provide savings to real economic investors again as its main task, it must of course be further feared that with monetary restraint by the central banks the economic situation will be strangled or aggravated by re-regularisation of the bank activities. This is also a reason, why

[137] Look: *Wann kommt die von Politikern und vielen Wirtschaftswissenschaftlern erwartete Inflation?* in: Unkonventionelle… (I), p. 45ff.

the re-regularisation of the bank commercial activities only makes headway hesitantly and the banks and finance service providers can continue their vicious activities.

Therefore the monetary policy must be released from the captivity as a hostage of the capital market. Thereby, the disturbing situation should be removed of the banks using the cheap central bank money since the crisis with an interest of nearly 0% for capital market transactions with high profits. For, after the intentions of the central banks, the low interest payment should only stimulate the real economy. So it is advisable to organise the monetary policy anew. With it the central banks could make also a contribution to the renovation of the public finances and the capital market.

For that purpose the money market should be organised as follows:

1. Separation of the bank system in capital market (investment banks) and commercial banks
2. Restriction of the possibility of commercial banks refinancing themselves at central banks
3. Monetary care of the economy by direct open market policy of the central banks without intercalation of private banks
4. Restriction of the public indebtedness on central bank loans
5. Specific selling of the gold reserves of the central banks to takeover Government stocks.

These proposals are to be understood as a bouquet where the single measures are interlinked.

1. Separation of the Bank System in Investment Banks and Commercial Banks

The universal bank system, as it exists, for example, in Germany, was unproblematic so long as the banks felt responsible to the real economy, granted their loans rather after substance value than after earning powers, and capital market transactions played a minor part. In the USA the investment banking had a bigger importance for a longer time. So that the real economy should not-like in particular after the worldwide economic crisis of 1929 be affected by the investment banking, the investment banking was separated in the USA by law from the normal commercial banking.

The >>Banking Act called the Glass-Steagall Act prescribed the introduction of a divided bank system, so an institutional separation between the classic deposit and lending business and the security business. Owing to the strong integration and interlinking between the investment and commercial banking, the banks suffered massive losses on the security side by price falls as well as on the credit side by loan failures during the bank crisis from 1929 to 1933, and at that time it should have been sure via separation that these events do not recur again.[138] [139] <<[140]

The fact that investment banking and commercial bank activity are two different business divisions can already be seen in the fact that also German banks separate the areas and split, for example, even the bank itself. Thus the *Deutsche Bank* separated the business division for the payment transactions and private customers in a so-called *Bank 24*. Wikipedia writes: >>On 1 September 1999 the Deutsche Bank AG outsourced the private customer and branch division and transferred it in the *Bank 24,* which was renamed at the same time in the *Deutsche Bank 24 AG* and looked after 6.8 million customers. While the wealthy private customers were excluded from the spin-off, the branches were at the same time renamed in the *Deutsche Bank 24*.<<[141] >>Enlarged by the business clients division, since the 1st of October the DB24 is called, 2002 *Deutsche Bank Private Clients and Business Clients AG* <<[142].

This splitting has also recently found its expression in the naming of two successors for the chairman of the board of Deutsche Bank Josef Ackermann. From both areas it was named a personality as a successor. If the successful new chairman of the board from investment banking, the Indian Anshu Jain would speak German, he possibly would already have been appointed the sole chairman of the board because of the weight, the investment banking had in the German bank.

Due to the experiences that the axiom turned out wrong that monetary increase causes inflation in each case, the money flowed primarily on the capital market, and there was therefore no more reason to put chains on the capital market.

Moreover, because financial services were regarded as the coronation of advanced business development, it was therefore recommended that financial services in particular should be promoted. Thus the Glass-Steagall Law, the separation of investment banking and commercial bank and loan business, became lifted in 1999. Since then the investment banks of the USA could make use of commercial deposits and private savings of the commercial division for capital market activities.

---

[138] Randall P. Kroszner; Raghuram G. Rajan: *The Role of Firewalls in Universal Banks: Evidence from Commercial Bank Securities Activities before the Glass-Steagall Act*, University of Chicago George G. Stigler Center for Study of Economy and State, Chicago, 1994.

[139] Ann-Kristin Achleitner: *Handbuch Investment Banking*, Gabler Verlag, 2002, P. 6.

[140] http://de.wikipedia.org/wiki/Glass-Steagall_Act.

[141] http://de.wikipedia.org/wiki/Deutsche_Bank_Privat-_und_Gesch%C3%A4ftskunden.

[142] loc. cit.

The financial crisis has shown that financial services and capital market yield very high profits, but are only partly of any use to the real economy and unfold rather a considerable sturgeon potential for the real economy. Therefore it's time to counteract again and distribute both business divisions to different bank types. Investment banks then cannot use and lose any more savings and commercial deposits in commercial banks by gambling with capital market transactions. Then the state must only guarantee the deposits of the commercial banks after the *Deposit Protection Fund*, financed by the banks themselves.

So commercial banks do not stand under the pressure any more to effect at short notice very lucrative capital market transactions to avoid too strong a drop in their earning power and to thus become takeover candidates for capital market sharks.[143] To act as investment bankers, German state banks have also surpassed their capability, as everybody knows, with market transactions. If necessary, commercial banks should be organised as corporations of public law or as co-operatives.

2. Refinancing at the Central Banks should be restricted to commercial banks

The central banks usually give central bank money to the banks which sell or pledge for it foreign currency and securities to the central banks. Because the banks have acquired the foreign currency and securities from their customers or from the capital market, the central bank money flows furthermore into the economy. The banks earn the interest difference between self-granted loans and the refinancing with central bank money.

The less this difference is, the less the banks earn or the higher the central banks fix their interest rate for the refinancing, the more the banks charge their customers again, indeed, of course only up to the amount that customers are ready to pay interest. If the bank customers do not want any more loans under the given conditions or the customers are not loan-worthy to the banks any more, the grant of credit falters and less central bank money is asked for at the central bank.

Then the granting of credits stagnates or even shrinks. But also the circulating currency supply stagnates or shrinks. Because the central banks are responsible primarily for the fact that the economy has enough necessary liquidity for payment processes, they manipulate the interest rate for refinancing credits to prevent liquidity narrowness or inflation caused by too high a money supply.

If the economy stagnates for lack of liquidity because, for example, as after the last crisis, the banks have suffered high losses and must reduce their monetary creation (banks must keep for monetary creation a certain amount of equity), then

143 See: *Wie Unternehmenskultur zur Shareholder Value Mentalität und Kapitalisten zu Heuschrecken wurden*, in: Unkonventionelle ...(I), p.69ff.

the central bank can feel constrained to turn up the supply of money as was the case in the last crisis, and lower the interest rate for the banks further to close to zero percent.

The central banks of course do not want to stimulate more speculations with their policy of cheap and easy money, but rather stabilise the real economy. Then universal banks, that is: investment banking and commercial bank activities combined, feel tempted of course to use the cheap possibilities to refinance primarily capital market games because they promise a higher profit. It is therefore recommendable to separate commercial banks and investment banks and that the central banks only offer the possibility of refinancing to the commercial banks.

Then the investment banks depend only on own customer payments and emitted bank loans to finance financial transactions, and cannot finance speculations with money from the central bank any more. Citizens, who entrust their money to the capital market and do not save at commercial banks, must then bear the full risk for their investments, as far as the investment banks themselves have not built up insert protection funds. The state should only guarantee, in any case, the inserts of the commercial banks, as far as their deposits are not already secured by Deposit Protection Funds.

3. Monetary supply of the economy by direct open market policy of the Central Banks without mediation of private banks

A restriction of the monetary supply of the economy via the refinancing of the banks is not sufficient to supply the economy with sufficient liquidity, and in particular not in times where the real economy stagnates. It stagnates above all because the savings rate is too big worldwide, especially because of the unequal distribution of income, and profit-promissory innovations and investments firstly do not keep up with the disproportionate growing savings volume and secondly are not worthwhile because of the accordingly lower consumption rate. Therefore, we have by height of the worldwide unemployment unused human production capacities and in few countries with higher employment, like Germany, increasingly precarious working relations. Accordingly the consumption expenditures are low.

Because under these circumstances real-economic investments are only a little worthwhile, only few savings are used for them. Therefore, in a stagnant real economy enough liquidity in the form of central bank money cannot be asked for. If only the former are allowed to refinance at the central banks after a separation of the bank system in commercial banks and investment banks, the liquidity supply of the economy could be too low. So the central banks additionally to the refinancing of the commercial banks must pursue so-called open market policies, that is: purchase and sell securities on the capital market and thus additionally pump in or withdraw money out of the economy.

Central banks pursue open market policies as a rule via private banks. This is also valid for the purchase and sales of state loans by the central banks. Thereby too close a relationship between state and central banks should be prevented, because in that case one fears that the state could borrow money from the central bank without restraint. However, on the other hand, it is not justified that the banks earn with open market politics.

The danger that states simply fall back on their central bank for additional state expenses, and borrows wanted additional money without limits, must be banished of course. This danger dwindles however, to such an extent, in which the states submit to a debt brake. In addition, the central banks must remain independent and may give loans to the state only in line with monetary-political necessities.

4. Liberation of the states from the stranglehold of the markets by restriction of the public indebtedness on Central Bank loans as means of the monetary supply of the economy

The real cause of the increasingly threatening state bankruptcies (and the expected bank crises and monetary crises stemming from it) are, that:

1. state expenses are raised too frivolously, and
2. states have financed necessary public expenses not by sufficient tax rises, but by public debt admissions. If one would have raised the tax so straight that in particular, those would have been met, who had purchased the state loans and of whom the provision for old age was already secured, a overextension of the states would not have happened and the standard of living of the these persons would also not have been affected.

The *markets* were additionally fed by the public indebtedness instead of financing the expenditures from taxes, and the states have made themselves dependent on the *financial markets*.

In the past, the *financial markets* have counted on the fact that states cannot become insolvent. However, they have overlooked that the money taken up by the states was used primarily for state expenses, that is consumption expenses in the form of public salaries, defence etc., in particular, however, also for transfer payments to needy persons, who are in a great measure victims of the unequal distribution of income, and that they flow again into the economy and therefore that state bonds are not based on real securities.

They have also not sufficiently taken into account that due national debts as a rule in each case are paid back from new indebtedness, so practically only revolve. The *snowball system*: Repayment of old debts and net new indebtedness from new indebtedness could have gone on endlessly if the financial markets had been ready to join in further games.

However, rating agencies were suddenly believed to have found out that countries as Greece cannot pay back their debts and so to them no revolving plus net new loans should be granted.

But no state pays back debts from running income – not just Greece. Japan is far higher indebted with more than 200% of the gross domestic product than Greece, and will never pay back its debts from running income but also only revolve the debts.

To whom it would be served, by the way, if the states really would pay back their debts from running income? What would the believers make of it, as by now they even cannot invest all running savings in the real-economy?[144] But although at maturity of debts Greece needs far less new credits in volume than, for example, Japan, and there is still enough capital looking for investment possibilities, Greece was found not worthy to get further loans.

After the look of the *financial markets* at the real value of the public state loans was sharpened, the high indebtedness of the other states, which had still inconceivably risen paradoxically because of the financial crisis, also struck them, so that one state after the other up to the United States was downgraded as less creditworthy.

Now the policies must count on the more realistic assessment of the national debts on the part of the financial markets. Nevertheless, the policy with hectic activity and insufficient measures tries to be able to satisfy the wishes of the financial markets. Because the states

- by this activity, however, pile up even more and more debts,
- transfer the existing public indebtedness of the countries only on others instead of cancelling them by insolvencies,
- if, like in Greece, debt cuts become unavoidable, these are not executed far enough,
- strangle the economy by economy measures,

and so do not calm the financial markets, and so the *markets* will be set more and more into panic mode over and over again.

[144] See: *Was machen die Gläubiger der Staatsschulden wenn die Staaten ihre Ausgaben reduzieren und den Anlegern somit keine Staatspapiere mehr verkaufen oder sogar bestehende Schulden zurückzahlen?*, in: *Unkonventionelle Betrachtungsweisen* ... (I), pages 67ff.

The currencies and the international trade are also endangered by the menacing state bankruptcies. The stranglehold of the financial markets to the budgets and the monetary policy must be broken. For a detailed argumentation of the relation of the circulation of money to the circulation of goods, the monetary political measures necessary need to be understood.

Money originates from indebtedness. Money is an achievement promise. In a simple form money originates from the fact that somebody buys something from another and gives him for it a promise to pay, for example, in the form of a bill of exchange. If the exhibitor of the promise to pay is loan-worthy, the receiver of the debenture can use it for another payment again. Thus this debt promise can be used as a currency, until it is redeemed by the exhibitor through an achievement again.

Central bank money originates from the fact that receivers of payment promises exchange these via commercial banks to the central bank in central bank money. Therefore, central bank money is just a promise to pay - originally on respective exchange in gold -. However, in the meantime, central bank money is valid just in itself as worth-containing because owners expect from central bank money that others accept it as currency.

On the other hand, therefore, the circulating amount of the central bank money depends on the indebted readiness of private persons and/or the state on the one hand, and the readiness of the central bank to exchange debt obligations of others in central bank money on the other side.

Because money has no real value in itself, but only numbers and mediates a debt, the sum of the real debt relations is not also synonymous with the amount of the circulating money. Only as far as debts were documented and are used as currency, are they really money. Somebody can receive an achievement from another and has got into debt in this respect. If he cannot compensate the achievement with own real achievement, he needs money. For, money as a debenture can be used to pay real debt obligations, and thus serves payment transactions. It substitutes further barter processes, which would be necessary to pay, for example, to purchase bananas if the buyer has only carrots as an equivalent which the buyer of the bananas does not need, however. So the supplier of carrots would then have to search for other buyers, who would give him products as an equivalent which the seller of the bananas would then accept as payment.

So the coming into existence and the disappearance of money must be regarded under other points of view, rather than that the production and the consumption of economic goods, although money is used for the distribution of the goods. For, if there is no liquidity for payments, an economy breaks down.

In respect of the optimum money supply of the economy the central banks should not become dependent on the fact that the banks and private persons and companies are interested enough to demand additional money. We have found out how the monetary supply of the economy was endangered, because it shrank after the crisis because the banks had to restrict their credit creation after their losses and enterprises and private persons paid back their debts as far as possible. The liquidity narrowness was so big that for its increase the American Central Bank President Bernanke suggested to throw down money from airplanes if necessary. So also to stimulate the banks to additional indebtedness, and via them the economy, the banks generously granted liquidity with an interest rate of nearly 0%. But, because the banks primarily financed capital market transactions with it again, the private sector, nevertheless, was not supplied with enough loans.

If however, the central banks are quite ready to offer money at virtually 0% of interest to get a sufficient monetary supply, why then not directly to the states? Why should the states borrow money from private banks at high interest, when they possibly could have got cheap central bank currency?

To that the following statements: As a matter of fact the economy cannot function without money. Nevertheless, real-economic processes follow laws other than the monetary creation, and both processes therefore should not be fused with each other.

The issue of money by the central bank is, for example, no grant of credits, as it is if somebody lends savings to another. Of course in both cases an equivalent is usually pledged. But by height of the savings must be invested, and must be bought corresponding to the savings. Otherwise stagnation threatens. Money must be made available against it by the height of the liquidity needed by the economy and that depends:

- on the velocity of the money, that is how many payment processes are effected in a time unit with it,
- the liquidity preference of the enterprises and citizens. How much money is hoarded and also
- what the money is used for. Thus we already saw that today the liquidity need is very high for capital market transactions, so that an immediate correlation money = real-economic purchase is not given any more.

Nevertheless the money produced by the money creator works as other circulating goods, and the money creator is the central bank, but in a broader sense the state. So the equivalent of the central bank money creation should also run to-wards the state, that is: central bank loans should be of benefit preferentially for the states, indeed, not by height of the need announced by the states, but only in harmony with an optimum monetary supply of the economy. Therefore an independent central bank cannot be renounced.

By restriction on open market policy the monetary supply can also be better uncoupled from economic and speculative developments, and the money supply policy can become more effective.

To the extent in which the central banks do not grant cheap refinancing credits to the banks or acquire debentures from them for the purpose of the money supply, but instead buy Government stocks or take them from the market, they thus reduce the public debts in respect to private creditors and contribute thus to the disencumberment of the states, and the favourable interest is of benefit for the states and with it the public welfare. Insofar in the currency-political discussion those are right who plead for the takeover of Government stocks by the central bank as a contribution to the solution of the debt crisis.

Of course central bank loans should only be granted to the states under serious monetary-political points of view, and also only as so-called *fresh money*, never for the repayment of old debts. Provided that government stocks are bought by the central bank at the capital market, it should happen as a rule at the actual price that is at the price which the threatened loans still have. For, the central bank must pay attention to the fact that it does not contribute itself to the stabilisation of ailing state loans and drag out necessary debt cuts.

Against the real statutes of the European central bank the takeover of ailing Government stocks is already carried out, indeed, to the stabilisation of the prices of the ailing government stocks. Until there are enough instruments to meet state bankruptcies, this practice may be justified temporarily. However, in the medium term it must be aimed that the public debts disappear by:

- a debt barrier,
- a debt cut,
- repayment via revenues from property deliveries,
- the suggested change of the monetary supply policy: instead of refinancing of the banks and
- direct grant of credits of the central banks to public authorities.

4.1 Which measures are necessary, that the economy does not collapse in the process of this conversion?

A rescue screen is needed for threatened banks, which have become saturated with needy government stocks, and will suffer such high losses with a debt cut that they will get over-indebted themselves or cannot exercise or are no more capable to exercise their bank functions because of too little equity.

So-called *Euro safety nets* were already created to stabilise the currency market and which should also support needy banks. The *Tagesspiegel* writes: >>In fact there are three versions of *Euro safety nets*: first the *European Finance Stabilisation Facility (EFSF)* in May, 2010 adopted by the European heads of state and heads of government; secondly ... the "enlarged" EFSF with new competence as the takeover of state loans; and thirdly the *European Stability Mechanism (ESM)*. In the ESM it shall also be obligingly regulated how private believers – banks and assurances – can be charged with the cost in the case of insolvency of a euro-country. Such a regulation is absent up til now. The lasting safety net ESM should substitute the EFSF from the middle of 2013; however, Minister of Finance Wolfgang Schäuble has already brought a former start into the play.<<[145]

Because it is desirable for the national debts to disappear and, therefore, the public debts be redeveloped primarily by debt depreciation, it shall be the primary job of the ESM to stabilise banks which are relevant for the system of the economy.

As it is within the public interest, state loans must be taken from the market and responsible bridging loans must be granted to the states, thus it should be as demonstrated rather the job of the central banks, unless the ESM itself is run as a bank, or in close collaboration with and with refinancing by the European Central Bank. But, the support to needy banks should be limited on the backup of the functioning of the banking activities in favour of the real economy. So the bank support should be based on the following principles:

1. Takeover (and/or if necessary nationalisation) of threatened banks relevant for the economic system to the given share prices. So a debt cut is realised.
2. Splitting of the banks into investment banks and commercial banks.
3. Return to morality based bank consultation. Banks must perform their work primarily in the interest of the customers of the banks, not to optimise the profits of the stockholders on account of the bank customers.
4. Reduction of the reimbursements of the bank employees, in particular the investment banker, to reasonable amounts, as the salaries of the management were limited to €500,000 and bonuses were particularly taxed in what happened with the last state participation in banks.

   Bank managers, such as Josef Ackermann, claimed to only be able to sign on investment bankers with the astronomical reimbursements having become common in the financial branch. Thus in the meantime new co-chairman of the board of the Deutsche Bank, Anshu Jain, earned €12,000,000 in 2010 as an investment banker. However, the German bank can no longer be a model for future banking.[146] A new bank ethics might be also estimated by investors who do not want to just play.
5. Reorganisation of the commercial banks, if possible into cooperatives or corporations of law.

   The *financialisation* of the economy has led to the fact that shares are not valued any more according to their substance value, but exclusively their capitalised earnings. Moreover according to the *shareholder value principle* the only task of the banks should be the profit maximisation for the stockholders. Bank managers were thereby forced to lead the

---

145 Miriam Schröder, Albrecht Meier: *Das ABC der Schuldenkrise*, in Der Tagesspiegel Number 21 119, 8.10.2011, p. 2.

146 Siehe: *Ist die Vergütung von Managern mit mehreren Millionen pro Jahr wirtschaftsethisch vertretbar?*, in. *Unkonventionelle ...* (I), p. 87ff.

employees to generate a very high earning power, also at the expense of an adequate equity of the company. If they did not do this, banks ran the risk of being taken over from competitors. From this point of view Josef Ackermann aimed to gain a 25-percent company equity yield, as it was also viewed as protection against hostile takeovers. At least this pressure must be taken away from the commercial banks, and for them *cooperatives* or *corporations of public law* offer suitable social structures.

The state means to be paid to the ESMF and guarantees (autumn, 2011), a total of 780 billion euro (from which only a portion is left because of the aid already granted), should be extended by a leverage with loans on about a billion euro. It is intended to guarantee 20-30% of the value of new debts of loan threatened states.

In respect of the volume of the European state debts, which are in danger of revolving, this measure cannot even be compared to one damming a dangerous water flood. For, water runs off sometime. However, the circulating state loans are only preserved as a danger. If the dam breaks then the ESMF, and with it the European states have to bear in the next crisis as planned 20 or even 30 percent of the national debt depreciation. Whether the 780 billion state means and guarantees are sufficient in that case, is very doubtful.

It is also surprising with which naivety politicians, as Wolfgang Schäuble, assume that the indebtedness crisis will disappear by itself by 2021 by this embankment and debt braking. In view of the deeper causes shown for the economic and financial crisis, which are fed by the unequal distribution of property and income and from it the new savings pressing on the capital market, and the dangers from the remaining world-economic imbalances, it would be a miracle in our fast moving time if the dam would hold for a longer period.

5. Selected sale of gold reserves of the Central Banks to buy Government stocks

Since time immemorial gold is regarded as an ideal form of money, although in the course of business development gold became less and less important as a circulating currency. After the pure gold currency, paper money was covered in gold with the result that, if a central bank's gold reserves dwindled, the central bank would also have to reduce the monetary supply. But that would still aggravate economic crises.

After both world wars the European countries had lost so much gold that they had to give up the gold reserve system. After the Second World War the US dollar became the world currency on account of the agreements of Bretton Woods on the 1st of July, 1944, because the US central bank committed itself to exchange US dollars any time for a fixed price of 35 USD/ ounce in gold.

Then in the course of the constant American balance of payment deficits, the USA also felt constrained to give up the obligation to change currencies in gold. Today the central banks of the countries again dispose of substantial gold reserves. However, gold bars in the bank safety deposits are of no use to anyone.

In countries with flexible currency exchange rates the exchange rate is the result of offer and demand, and in countries with firm exchange rates no country can or will hoard foreign currency of devaluation-threatened countries in order to exchange it in gold at the concerned central bank. Whether a country has therefore a lot of or few gold bars in the safe deposit, no longer plays a role for international payments.

However, because gold is still regarded highly by private persons and is supposed to be stable in value and is bought particularly in crisis periods, the gold price is thereby forced up, thus the central banks have the chance to contribute to the disencumberment of the states through gold sales for the purpose of buying Government stocks.

When the gold price is very high, the central banks should therefore sell gold and purchase needy government stocks with the proceeds. Extraordinary profits will be realised by height of the lower price of the stocks due to their downgrading on account of the previous owners of the government stocks, and by height of the difference of the actual gold price to the previous purchase price of the gold. By 2012, the gold price has risen to 1.668,60 USD.[147]

The central banks should then exchange the needy government stocks they bought to the state which has issued them, against nearly interest-free state loans. Eventually, the debts can be completely erased by the profit from the gold sales. For the monetary supply of the economy, this exchange action gold against Government stocks would be neutral if the central banks pay for the government stocks just as much as they get for the gold sales.

If very high profits should be made from the gold sales, the gold sales should be measured of course, so that the price does not sink too much. But even, if the gold price should sink in the course of these sales, the action can still make sense, at least up to the gold price of the stored gold bars.

A renovation of public finances by gold sales also has the welcome side effect that the gold circulation increases, and the chances rise that gold is used for jewelers and other uses and thus pleases the people.

---

[147] See: http://www.gold.de/goldpreisentwicklung.html.

V. The growing unequal distribution of property and income and their impact on the economic welfare and social peace

Distribution of the Individual* net-property in Germany		
Distribution Criteria	**2002**	**2007**
Poorest 10%	-1,2	-1,6
10-20%	0,0	0,0
20-30%	0,0	0,0
30-40%	0,4	0,4
40-50%	1,3	1,2
50-60%	2,8	2,8
60-70%	7,0	6,0
70-80%	11,8	11,1
80-90%	19,0	19,0
Wealthiest 10%	57,9	61,1

* Persons in Private Households with Age 17 Years and more. Portion of the Whole in Percent. Sources: SOEP; Calculations DIW Berlin. DIW Berlin 2009

The current movement of incomes and property in favour of a few becomes an ever increasing danger to social peace. It is increasingly recognised as a social problem. However, the unequal distribution of income and property is measured in postulated justice norms which are opposed to those who regard the unequal income and property distribution as a result of professional capacity of economic operators, or market liberals even believe, particularly in America and Europe that the more concentrated income and property is amongst a few, the more will be invested and the economy will flourish.

Nevertheless, it might have become clear from the present arguments that an unequal distribution of income injures not only an abstract justice ideal, but is also the economic cause for the crisis susceptibility of our economy, and the present economic and financial crisis. For, the unequal distribution of income and property causes:

1. a *trend increasing depression danger*, as far as savings find no real economic investment possibilities and/or capital at the capital market it is therefore burnt by speculations and income of finance service providers[148].

[148] If state loans are bought with savings, the money, as far as it is used for state expenses, becomes consumption again economically, and is classed as *burnt* as savings. In the course of capital market transactions income always results for the finance service providers which will also to a certain extent flow into consumption. False profits from price increases

2. an *increasing state indebtedness*, as far as states prevent depression dangers by economic stimulus programs and/or, particularly in the USA, by flooding the economy with money.
   As far as no real-economic investments are released by the flooding with money, the speculation will of course be promoted whereby economical savings can again be burnt.
3. an *increasing state indebtedness*, as far as a reverse of the unequal distribution of income due to the deindustrialisation and increasing unemployment and sinking wage level, lower income subscribers become impoverished and force the states to rise social expenses and these are not financed by accordingly higher inland revenues.
4. *foreign trade imbalances*. To the extent that produced goods cannot be sold by the home anymore and too few goods can be imported because of too low consumption, so goods and capital must be exported. Active trade balances occur and by the same height passive trade balances of other countries with corresponding indebtedness of these countries.
   If as a result other countries and/or public households become insolvent, those receivables must be written off or be taken over from other states. If the claims are held against foreign states by banks as usual, and these are endangered by a devaluation of the claims themselves, the states can be charged further for the renovation of the banks. The public indebtedness can thereby increase dramatically, as experiences have shown.
5. *Disturbance of the real economy by speculations in raw materials and currencies.* Fleeting capital which finds no real-economically sensible gainful investment possibilities turned more and more to play money for which finance service providers invented new and more ingenious capital market games and still do.
   The capital market games also speculate from raw materials important for the real economy to food and thereby unfold a considerable economic sturgeon potential. This is also the case for the speculations both against and in currencies. Also if currencies are bought, because they are regarded as having a high worth, the exchange rate of a currency can be forced up in such a way, as for example in autumn, 2011 the Swiss franc, that the export possibilities of the country are endangered and cheap imports affect the home industry.

The unequal distribution of income therefore turns out to be the central problem for the renovation of the economy, regardless of some justice considerations.

---

of assets also partially become consumption expenses. As long as the prices of assets rise, the investors still register a profit. However the losses will be realised when the prices of assets fall again.

A row of absorption measures was recommended for the settlement of these inequalities, such as:

1. Devaluation of public debts in cases of state bankruptcy
2. Rise of the taxes and deliveries up to transaction taxes and death taxes
3. Sales of currency gold for the buying of Government stocks.

However, these measures can have considerable side effects interfering with the economy, and tax rises only diminish fleeting capital in the long term and the corresponding believer's positions of the national debts. So the public finances should be globally redeveloped at short notice by a unique *property delivery*, as it was described above.

By a similar measure Solon removed the debt slavery of Greek citizens around 600 B.C. and at that time restored the economy and the social peace in Athens[149]. Maybe it is a sign of history that the present debt crisis also started with Greece.

Anyone should be able to see that the unequal distribution of income was a cause of the financial and economic crisis, and it is only seriously picked out as a central theme by leftist parties and – remarkably by wealthy people. As economic competence is hardly granted to leftist parties in public discussion because of the breakdown of the socialist planned economy, we want to provide a forum here to the co-initiator of the *Initiative of Wealthy Persons for a Property Levy*, Dieter Lehmkuhl.

In a contribution to the Tagesspiegel Dieter Lehmkuhl justified the need of a property levy in a unique way, and with his permission this contribution is printed here.

>>Wealth and Justice

We experience a new justice debate. With the ideologically motivated concept of "Social envy", the subject of the growing social inequality has been attempted to be dismissed for years. This is not possible any more. The facts are unequivocal. During the last 10 years the income inequality and poverty has increased more with us than in almost any other OECD country. Moreover the rapid increase is frightening. The case is the same for property distribution. The upper 10% of the population own 63% of the property in Germany, and after deduction of the self-inhabited real estate it could even be up to 75%. For the first time in the history of the Federal Republic it has come to a polarisation of the incomes, i.e. the big incomes increase, while the middle and lower net incomes sink really: since 2000 it's been about 15% in the lower tenth of the population. The ability of individuals to accumulate such a large amount of private wealth

[149] *Eine Solonische Entschuldung der öffentlichen Hände*, in: Unkonventionelle Betrachtungsweisen…(I) p. 109ff.

should be evaluated less as expression of competent commercial sense, but more as a failure of the society to form a fair economy", as one says in the Alternative World Health Report (GHW2).

This concentration of private wealth in the hand of a relative few goes along with growing private and public poverty. The results of it are impoverishment, soup kitchens, people who live eating out of garbage cans, educational poverty, neglect of the infrastructure, restriction of public duties in education, ecology and clear incisions in the social nets. The bank rescue programs for which means are now indefinitely made available which were used before for urgent social duties now just aggravate the situation. The well-to-do and banks, who have profited during the boom phase of the financial market speculation, and whose property was protected by the rescue packages, up to now remain spared, and profit again from the public indebtedness.

The question arises, why the growing inequality has only now become a subject of public interest, although the data was given about it some time ago. The sociologist and poverty researcher *Butterwege* gives the answer: „Because at least the rich and super-rich have no interest in a radical change of income relations, property relations and rule relations, the public decisively influenced by them struggles against a truth that financial market capitalism has generated more poverty than necessary, or the truth that a modern industrial state such as the Federal Republic would be able to remove them if it were politically willing to do it". The late US author Upton Sinclairs formulated in a similar manner: „It is very difficult to bring a person, to understand something if his salary depends on the fact that he does not understand."

Till the middle of the seventies the Federal Republic was still a relatively egalitarian country. The social stratification of the society more resembled an onion rather than a pyramid, with relatively small classes of wealthy and poor persons in the upper resp. lower edges of the society. Not only the wide middle class, the "stabiliser" of the society, but also persons from the lower classes were entitled to have hopes for a social rise. Nearly all classes took part in the productiveness progress. In the meantime, the middle class eroded and its members were threatened by real descent fears. A large part of the young generation will foreseeably live materially under worse conditions than their parents. Also well qualified will increasingly have to work in precarious employment. Thus in respect to the saying „Achievement needs to become economically remunerative again ".

How did it come so far? Mainly by a tax policy which favours high incomes, property, inheritances and enterprises unilaterally, but relatively increasingly imposes the middle class as well as lower incomes, by tax rate and social security contributions, as well as by rise of indirect taxes. A study of the economist Gerd Grözinger of the University of Flensburg which compares the tax and delivery rate of 15 old EU countries (in % of the GDP) points: If we would only pay as many taxes, as the average of these countries, we would have €100 billion / year more in inland revenue in the public households. The lowest taxes of all, relevant for distribution, are in Germany, i.e. those which burden the well to do by their progressive rate relatively more. Earlier the rich and enterprises carried a clearly higher portion of the tax burden. In the meantime, the relations have turned. Also the incomes, in particular in the economy, have developed apart quite crassly. If former managers and bosses earned 20-40 times more than employees/workers of their company, it is today a multiple of it. In the USA the manager with the highest remuneration earns around 300,000 fold (!) of the minimum wage there. That, as well as the banker's bonuses, shows a severe imbalance. The rules of the game, which led to these astronomical incomes, were simply changed.

What has that to do with justice? That is in line neither with the teachings of the big philosophers as Platon, Aristotelis, Augustin, Kant, John Rawls or important economists as Adam Smith or the Indian economic Nobel Prize Laureate Amartya sen, nor with the ethics of the world religions and the inheritance of the clarification.

About what justice is can be argued splendidly. Nevertheless, most people have a deep feeling for injustice: Big social inequality, growing poverty in a rich country, gigantic bonuses for speculators and salaries, which no achievement justifies, injure the justice feeling of most people, almost everywhere in the civilised world. This also applies for huge profits from capital assets which originate without any own contribution and which are taxed lower, in the meantime, by the capital payment tax than many by hard work and who earn achieved incomes. It is also regarded as unfair that flourishing enterprises aim at an indecent capital yield of 20-25% and release manpower, or in spite of high profits, move their locations in low wage countries. The sense of justice is also injured because owing to varied tax breaks and "tax creation possibilities" the 400 richest households pay only 35% of taxes on their gross income (the uppermost 10% in the country only 25 %), although the top rate of income tax is 45%.

So it is not surprising if only a few people think that we still have fair play on the whole within our country. Nevertheless, (social) justice should mean that strong shoulders are just stronger burdened. Earlier this solidarity maxim was quite predominantly valid as consensus. We have said goodbye to this consensus, in the meantime, to a greater extent. But what does such an eroding solidarity mean for us living together? Bigger (income) equality serves the well being of all, as nearly all investigations of developed countries show. This confirms not only the look at the Scandinavian countries. Hence, social justice is not only an order of morality, but also the political and economic reason. It strengthens the trust in a society without which a prosperous life together or a stable economy is hardly conceivable.

“The economy needs new values“ is the name of a book of the Austrian economic journalist Christian Felber, which clears up many myths. How true!

As the Basic Law puts it in article 14 (2): „Property obliges. Its use should serve the welfare of the general public at the same time“. This maxim as a gradation has also got lost to a great extent. It is time that we all observe that policy again.<<[150]

The conversion of state debts could be reduced so far by a property levy that state bankruptcies and speculations against single currencies could be turned away. For, state bankruptcies have a lot of undesirable side effects. One thinks of the banks so affected by it which must devalue the government stocks held by them, and can thereby come into financial difficulties and must be stabilised then by the states.

Because Government stocks are also bought preferentially from pension funds and life insurances and for the purpose of the provisions for old age, many small investors would also experience state bankruptcies, whilst a property levy will charge specifically wealthy people whose provision for old age is thereby not affected.

Thus those are also burdened who would have to bear the renovation of the public finances anyway. For it can strangle the economy, when reducing state expenses, which are of benefit for the destitute and the general public to repay creditors of national debts, because the believers of this money do not need it, unless for capital market speculations[151]. So the often used phrase, *we may not burden future generations, with public debts,* is misleading. Once debts are paid back, this is only possible when those which are taxed for the debt erasure were actually the believers of the government stocks before. The believers of the state loans also belong to the future generations[152], however they have not earned but inherited their property.

However, regardless of the renovation of the public finances, provisions must be also made to prevent a further movement of the incomes and property to the hands of only a few. Mechanisms must be created which preserve the social harmony. For this purpose, as explained above, those parts of income, which are used neither for consumption nor for real-economic investments, must be charged more with deliveries, namely as demonstrated with speculation taxes and death taxes.

Moreover death taxes are particularly important because they do not charge "top performers", as one used to say, but only their descendants who must still prove whether they are also *top performers,* and if not they have economic ethically no right that those born not rich in the future generations should pay back loans to them, which the forefathers granted for public duties.

---

[150] Dieter Lehmkuhl, co-initiator of the "Initiative of Wealthy Persons in favour of capital levy": *Property obliges!*, guest commentary in the *Tagesspiegel*, 25.01.2011

[151] See: *Was machen die Gläubiger der Staatsschulden, wenn die Staaten ihre Ausgaben reduzieren und den Anlegern somit keine Staatspapiere mehr verkaufen oder sogar bestehende Staatschulden zurückzahlen?* in: Unkonventionelle ...(I) , p.67ff.

[152] See: *Die gespaltene Generation*, in: Unkonventionelle ...(I) , p. 65.

By inheritance taxes (and this is also valid for donation taxes if what has been given is only a hidden inheritance), the start terms for future generations can be adapted again for each other. This should also make sense to liberal market ideologists, because no market economy can promote the public weal if a few have almost everything and so also receive almost all capital income, the majority, however, in a de-industrializing economy, compete only for less and less jobs and have no resources and reserves to start economic activities as an entrepreneur and to secure their standard of living.

Citizens are absolutely ready to give available means for necessary charitable tasks. This also shows the high donation amount in emergencies. With taxes many citizens often do not immediately see, however, what the taxes have been used for, and there are doubts if civil servants make sensible use of public revenue. This is also true of course if special deliveries should be raised from rich and wealthy people. Thus Harald Christ also says in a Spiegel interview: >>It is easier
for a wealthy person to pay higher taxes if he knows that the money is spent for sensible tasks.<<[153] Therefore it should be aimed a stronger integration of the citizens in decisions of public expenditures.

Moreover, the understanding must be awakened for the measures to overcome the perverted economic ethics which is a result of the *financialisation* of the economy. But new facilities and regulations to prevent economic undesirable trends are needed below higher revenues from higher income subscribers. *Casino capitalism* must be overcome and be developed into a *social liberal economic system.*

---

[153] Stefan Kaiser Spiegel interview with Ex-Banker and Multimillionaire Harald Christ: *Höhere Steuern für Vermögende*, 31.08.2011, http://www.spiegel.de/wirtschaft/soziales/0,1518,783640,00.html.

C. From the liberal to the social-liberal economic system

I. Liberal economic system as a base of our standard of living and its limits

Social development is based on the emancipation of the individuals from religious, social and natural dependence and their free development. The *spiritual* emancipation from religious restraint began with the *enlightenment*: from which the then modern science and technology originated, the *economic one*: with free trade and the *social one*: with the democratisation of policy.

These three emancipation forms are mutually caused by themselves. Without technical progress no new products and production forms can be developed. Without trade, goods cannot be distributed rationally and without state there is no order.

In estate-based society the economic behaviour of the people is still based on the community and on an order. People produce for others and expect an income befitting social standing.

Profit as a motive of economic action originated in particular in trade. He who pursues trade, only looks at what profit can be made by buying and reselling goods. With trade the emotional relationship to self-made products gets lost. Hence, traders were first regarded as travelling people standing outside the society, unless the society itself was a trading nation, as for example the Hanseatic towns. Then, however, trade was also based by befitting social norms. One spoke of a "*royal businessman*".

The estate based society was destroyed by traders who sold new products and induced the new production and distribution methods, and thereby developed the economy. This behavior was socially justified with the propagation of the *Free Market Economy* according to which the selfish striving of the single people is harmonised by the market and should optimally promote the whole welfare too.

The market ideology originally only determined the economic behaviour of traders, but then also became the motive of the producers who produced for trade or traded themselves. This behaviour pattern was even hypostatised to be the natural behaviour of every person. According to it: every person offers something and that he should get a high a yield as possible for his work. However, the fact went unnoticed, that

1. most people only want to have a job giving them satisfaction and the revenue to live and lead a social life in familiar surroundings and
2. there are still other motives as for example to serve the state or God, to help people as a doctor, to create pieces of art, to develop spiritually and morally, to pursue science and/or to form something politically socially and

3. trade would not function if others would not work to satisfy social needs.

Nevertheless, besides technical progress, we owe our current standard of living decisively to the profit oriented market economy.

The liberal market economy theory postulates the following maxims for the economic process in a simplified scheme:

1. The market mechanism provides for the fact that individual profit maximisation promotes the whole welfare at the same time, because a person can sell only his goods if others buy them for the quoted price.
2. Economic activities will make a distinction between: Work and consuming and saving and investing.
   According to the market economy theory the people, in the end, are only interested in consuming. Work is only an effort which must be done to procure oneself consumer goods. That is: work earns an equivalent. Saving is foregoing consumption, so also an arduousness task which must be paid an interest, or the savings are invested and the investor receives a profit as an equivalent.
3. the state should abstain from economic activities as far as possible and only guarantee the market rules.

These maxims should be critically scrutinised in view of historical experiences.

1. To what extent the does the market guarantees the whole welfare?

The condition required for the fact that the market can promote the whole welfare at the same time is that:

1. nobody has such a large amount of market power, that he is a monopoly that can determine the market price, or there are not just a few who come to an agreement with one another to manipulate the price.
   This danger is also recognised by market theorists and is fought with anti-monopoly and anti-cartel-political measures. Because of the legal requirement enterprise coalescences have to be approved, and the market power can really be limited. Cartel agreements, however, can only be prevented to a smaller extent. One only needs to observe the costs of petrol: all oil companies have nearly the same prices and on the same days. For example, on Mondays and on Thursdays when the prices are some cents lower. Free filling stations can only offer slightly lower prices because they are dependent on the same wholesalers and thus probably have no elbowroom.
   The salary structure it also often less determined by offer and demand, rather than by estate-related salary appointments. One thinks of the relations of government members, doctors, lawyers or even board members of big enterprises. The fact that the boards of directors of big

enterprises have such a high income also depends on the fact that representatives of the same caste are in the supervisory boards who have to decide the salaries.[154] This is also the case for the compensations, the so-called *golden handshake* if board members leave an enterprise. The Victory gesture of Josef Ackermann the former chairman of the board of the Deutsche Bank – was typical of it during the hearing about the legality of a special payment for the then chairman of the board of the Mannesmann AG, Klaus Esser, as Mannesmann was taken over from Vodafone.

In a referendum in March 2013 the Swiss already adopted a set of measures to overcome these ills. Inter alia was established, that the remunerations of managers have to be limited and are not to be decided by supervisory boards any more, but rather by the shareholders.

2. The market only adjusts offer and demand in the interest of the whole welfare if suppliers and buyers have widely the same market position and all have the same start chances.

   If, however, as today in Germany, a few own almost everything and also accordingly earn most of the income, the distribution of the goods is optimised purely concerning the buying power, but not however in respect of the whole welfare. Because of this imbalance, and the relatively higher savings rate of the higher income subscribers, the property distribution moves on and on in favour of just a few. At the same time thereby the danger crisis increases with the result that social peace is endangered more and more.

3. The market only adjusts offer and demand in the interest of the whole welfare if it is not disturbed by speculative capital market transactions. Speculations against single currencies and raw materials in particular affect the economy injuriously. These dangers are being increasingly recognised. The problems of the currency speculations, released by the menacing insolvency of Greece in 2010, endangered the euro zone and, in addition, the world economy. Action should also be taken against raw material speculation. The *Tagesspiegel* reported in October, 2011: >>The USA want to take a tougher line with the raw material markets, and limit speculation purchases. After a long debate on Tuesday (local time), the stock market supervision responsible for derivative trade CFTC dismissed a draft to regulate the trade of oil, metals and grain which would have radically changed the rules of the game. The quintessential point is the controversial proposal to limit the number of the contracts held by a trader. From these measures CFTC boss Gary Gensler promised a calming of the price trend. However, large parts of the branch do not want to allow such chains and warn that investments would then move away overseas to

[154] see: *Ist die Vergütung von Managern mit mehreren Millionen Euro pro Jahr wirtschaftsethisch vertretbar?,* in: Unkonventionelle ... (I), p. 87ff.

markets regulated less strictly. From the advocates of harder rules, speculators contribute a lot to the rise in price of crude oil or other raw materials and with it thus raise the costs for both industry and consumers. The group of 20 leading industrial countries and threshold countries (G20) also has a regulation of the raw material markets on the agenda.<<[155]

2. How sustainable are the liberal economic-theoretical definitions of producing and consuming and saving and investing?

According to the economic theory based on the liberal market economy ideology, *production* and *work* are: trouble and nuisance, which are only suffered because the person must procure means for consumption, either immediately or, if he saves the product or the equivalent of his work and invests it, to be able to consume more later on. So liberal economic theorists do not have any problem if, out of need, somebody is forced to work beyond his reserves of strength and/or change his work, the location and his native country to find work, or if even psychological illnesses increase.

Claudia Maier writes: >>Mental disturbances were the most frequent reason for people being unfit for work last year. If the portion of psychological illnesses was at 15 percent in 1993, it s t e a d i l y rose during the following years and reached around 40 percent in 2010. This was found out by the *German Pension Scheme* (DRV). In this respect it is notable that the people involved are younger and younger: In 1980 an incapacitated person was an average of 56 years, today they are only scarcely more than 50 years old. And the purely psychologically sick people are only 48.3 years.

This development does not surprise the chairman of the German Psychotherapist's Union *Dieter Best*. On one hand the professional life accelerates more and more, economic processes become more complicated and demands are higher. Ringing mobile phones, constant e-mails and the pressure of superiors are omnipresent. Above all a separation between occupation and private life is hardly possible any more for many employees, thanks to mobile devices. In addition the working hours are constantly rising.<<[156] Of course today psychological illnesses can be recognised earlier. However, that alone does not explain the increase.

The possibility is also blotted out that men can take pleasure in their work, that they see a purpose of life in their job. For, if one would include enjoyment on the job in the market model, those who are enjoying their work and find fulfilment in it would have to earn less. For, insofar they make no sacrifices.

---

[155] rtr: *USA schränken Spekulation mit Rohstoffen ein*, in: Der Tagesspiegel Nr. 21 131, 20.10.2011, p.22.

[156] Claudia Maier: *Psychisch krank in jungen Jahren*, in: Der Tagesspiegel Nr. 21 129,. 18.10.2011, p.16.

Accordingly those would have to earn more for whom work is only a tiresome drudgery. Nevertheless, it is actually the opposite: those who feel the greatest fulfilment in their work also have the highest yields.

If the enjoyment to work would be included, it would have to be asked with rationalisation about whether the destruction of jobs, and with it their chances to earn money, and their working satisfaction are offset by the higher salary of the capital owners and/or if the rationalisation leads to price-reduction of the product prices and additional consumer enthusiasm of the buyers of the products.

In a dynamic economy, in which as many jobs are released as new jobs are created via rationalisation, the decision might fall out in favour of rationalisation. If, however, no new jobs are to be expected and capital owners speculate at the capital market with additional profit by height of the saved labour cost, then the decision may be different.

Liberal economic theorists will argue against it that an enterprise cannot afford to renounce on rationalisation possibilities through release of workers because otherwise it is swept away from the market by the competition.

But this argument already shows that the market does not necessarily optimize the whole welfare, but rather only profit of those with economic and industrial power. So the absolution of the market is merely questionable and the economic policy must consider how injurious effects of the market can be prevented against the whole welfare of society.

As an example of such a conflicting aim, the discussion about the minimum wage may be looked at. Liberal economic theorists argue: If the wages do not fall enough in industrial countries such as Germany, then jobs will be outsourced to cheap labour countries. So these theorists accept that the affected persons must resign themselves to precarious employer-employee relationships, and thereby lose their self-worth because otherwise they would have to be supported by social help and could fall into poverty.

To liberal economic theorists it would have to be replied that these disadvantages of the market mechanism must be compensated by the appointment of a minimum wage, and if necessary by foreign trade controls. Furthermore the affected persons must be supported socio-politically because of the low chances to earn money. Thereby the tax burden increases again which, in the end, also meets those who as enterprisers profit from the cheap wages.

For the purpose of profit maximisation and rationalisation the market also accepts child employment, caged hens, environmental damage and the use of questionable food additions. The more complicated and uneasy the economic processes become to grasp, the more the market must be adjusted namely not only in order to keep away damages from society and nature, but also because the *market* has the trend to destroy itself more and more.

II. The role of the State in society and market economy

From the afore demonstrated, it has become clear that an uncontrolled market economy, in which the market participants are guided only towards the egoism, destroys itself and the society and how the state must intervene more and more with regulations and own actions in the market events. One need only think of the gigantic expenditures that let economically disadvantaged people take part in the social life.

The variety of duties of the state in the economic life have made the state the biggest trading partner, and have also caused an indebtedness which approaches the height of the gross domestic product if it has not already crossed this border. Japan already has a national debt of more than 200 percent of the gross domestic product.

Approximately 50 percent of the GDP is state-related and the efforts to overcome the casino capitalism can still increase the influence of the state on the economy considerably more. However, the state thus threatens to become a Moloch who suffocates individual action. How should this development be dealt with?

Certainly the liberal basic conviction is right that the state should only fix and guarantee the juridical frame, although today this is more complicated and many-sided, than in former times. However, the state can only avoid being involved in the economic process if economic behaviour of the market participants is not so selfish.

We need an area of society between ordering state and economic actions in the interest of individuals, in which citizens act in favour of private and non-profit interests being mediated with one another. This area is in principle nothing new. It already exists in the form of *parties to collective agreements*, *chambers of commerce, corporations of public law*, *foundations* and *associations*. Those kinds of social activities should be developed further. We call it a *Self-Administrating Economy*.

III. Mediation of private and state duties by self-administering institutions

Besides production and action led by profit interest on one hand, and the regulation of the market by the state on the other side, there is still the wide area of not for profit-related social institutions with educational, cultural and social objectives. The foundation of such institutions was originated by citizens and enterprisers who organised themselves in the form *of associations* and *organisations* or founded *endowment funds* and on the other hand from the state, which outsourced public duties in the form of *institutions* or *corporations of public law*. Institutions of public law are, for example, universities, schools and churches

1. Society-related private initiatives

Examples of society-related private initiatives are: Nature conservation associations and associations supporting social purposes, culture and sport and endowments.

Associations and endowments do not only promote social life; they are also financed immediately by the citizens and thereby relieve the state of duties. Hence, contributions and endowments up to now should be released as much as possible from tax charges. According to the principles of a social liberal society, private initiatives also rank before state organisation.

Unions with socio-political and economic interests, as parties of collective agreements, economic chambers, and others which regulate social and economic problems amongst other things both for themselves and others also belong to the society-related private initiatives.

1.1 Parties of Collective Agreements as regulators of the labour market

Because the labour market could not be optimally regulated by offer and demand and the states could not fix the wages themselves, the states felt constrained to admit trade unions, and with it of course employers' associations, and to entrust them with the regulation of the employer-employee relationships. Only when the trade unions are too weak to represent the interests of the employees does the state have to fix minimum wages, or prescribe compulsive membership in the trade union responsible for them, and for example, for the membership of enterprises in Chambers of Industry and Commerce or other chambers.

The German policy must still perform this job in order to harmonise the labour market. However, it must also make sure at the same time that special trade unions for single professional guilds are not able to create chaos at the labour market at the same time, as was the case in the UK before Margret Thatcher.

1.2 Economic Chambers

Self-government institutions of the economy were created for single professional guilds, which regulate everything that the professional guilds can regulate in the common interest, for example apprentice's education, issue certificates of origin, developing opinions of drafted legislative bills et cetera.

1.3 Associations authorised with public activities

The German *TÜV Technical Supervision Associations* are an example of how sovereign rights were transferred to private institutions. They have their origin based in the security need of the manufacturers of a steam boiler. Wikipedia writes: >>In the time of the industrialisation the owners of steam boilers founded independent regional supervision organisations in the form of associations, and which prevented accidents so successfully that from 1871 the membership in such an association was released from the inspection by a state inspector. Stemming from the increasing number and efficiency of steam engines, there had been more and more accidents by exploding (more exactly: detonating) steam boilers.

The new regional "Steam Boiler Technical Supervisory and Auditing Organisation" (DÜV), as self-help organisations of the steam boiler operators, thus became an early example of a very successful privatisation of state examinations. Because they were so successful with the accident prevention in the fast developing steam boiler technology field, they were later also authorized to carry out safety tests and security checks in other technical areas, e.g. recurring checks of automobiles, as well as in respect of driving licenses.<<[157]

2. Corporations and Institutions of Public Law

The state founded *corporations or institutions of the public law* with regards to where politics were interested in the participation of the economy and the citizens in society-related duties.

According to *Gabler's Economic Encyclopedia* >>an association of public law is an organisation which is fulfilling public tasks within or on behalf of a public authority under state supervision, and if necessary with sovereign means beyond the immediate state activities. Corporations of public law are legal entities, hence, can be subject to rights and duties, complain in their own name and be sued. They enjoy different prerogatives; their employees are officials and employees of the civil service. ... Examples: Municipalities, districts, local health insurance schemes, land assurance institutions, professional associations, law societies, medical associations, high-level schools.<< >> In the institutions of the public law they are otherwise organised as corporate institutions. <<[158]
>> In contrast to the corporation of public law, the institution of public law not is organised as a corporate institution<<. An institution of public law is >>an administrative body of public law which serves the fulfilment of certain public duties, e.g., libraries, schools etc. <<[159]

---

[157] http://de.wikipedia.org/wiki/T%C3%9CV.
[158] http://wirtschaftslexikon.gabler.de/Definition/koerperschaft-des-oeffentlichen-rechtp.html
[159] http://wirtschaftslexikon.gabler.de/Definition/anstalt.html.

A model for *institutions or corporations of public law* serving social interests can be public broadcasters in Germany.

2.1 The public broadcasters in Germany as a model for institutions or corporations of public law serving social interests

>>The form of the institution of the public law was chosen in the post-war period because, in the view of the west allies, it corresponded in a nearly ideal manner as a broadcasting company not controlled by the state or any social group. It can be entitled to the right of self-government and awarded prerogatives of charitable institutions, and so reaches a high degree of independence from the state. The activities of the radio companies are controlled by supervision committees (*Broadcasting Council, Administrative Council*) in which all socially relevant groups and organisations are represented.<<[160]

For all radio companies under public law in the Federal Republic of Germany, the *Broadcasting Council* is >>the representation of the general public and the highest supervision committee commissioned with program control (in the ZDF under the title of Television Council), which alone, on proposal of the administrative council or by common meeting with this council, determines the personnel management of the institution, director or board of directors.

The size of the committee is fixed very differently; it ranges from 26 members currently with radio Bremen up to 74 members in the SWR. How the members are elected, and the spectrum of organisations, groups and associations also vary. Predominantly the delegation beneficiaries are named in the respective broad-casting company law, and in more country institutions proportionally in respect of the federal countries involved. Besides, in the NDR and SWR partial committees are formed for the single countries (Country-Palatinate Network.), in the MDR the federal country groups. In general broadcasting company councillors are provided from both big confessions, the Jewish cult municipalities, employees and employers, representatives of parliaments or recently of parties as well as government representatives. The time of office for the broadcasting company councils is mostly four, five or six years.<<[161]

The Administrative Council is >>the second supervision committee after the *Broadcasting Council* in all public law radio companies of the Federal Republic. The *Administrative Councils* mostly have mostly seven or nine members–... – which are chosen exclusively or predominantly by the Broadcasting Council.... In some cases there are one to four – in the SWR seven – members who are sent by

[160] http://www.ard.de/intern/abc/-/id=1643802/nid=1643802/did=1657068/1k1ssy6/index.html#abcListItem_1657068.

[161] http://www.ard.de/intern/abc/-/id=1643802/nid=1643802/did=1657072/edf1ld/index.html#abcListItem_1657072

the state side or belong to the committee qua office, in other cases up to three representatives of the employees of the respective institution. The duties of the *Administrative Council* normally consist of checking the budgetary proposal and annual accounts, in concluding the contract of employment with the director and in supervising the management, however, the program control is explicitly excluded in some broadcasting companies of public law. Now and then the *Administrative Council* also has the right to suggest a director to the *Broadcasting Council*, or as in the SWR, participate in the election of him.<<[162]

Other institutions or corporations of public law are organised the same way. According to this model, as many social interests, as possible, should be out-sourced from the state and transferred into legally independent organisations. Because these organisations are financed by contributions and reallocations, the taxes which run immediately towards the state could decrease to the same extent. Furthermore the citizens would know which task they have to make contributions towards.

2.2 The further development of already existing institutions and corporations of public Law

Concerning the juridical structure and the duties of *institutions and corporations of public law,* there is probably hardly anything to improve except their financing and a stronger participation of the citizens. Let’s go through the single institutions and corporations of public law:

2.2.1 Social Security

The pension scheme, legal health insurances and unemployment insurance belong under “social insurances”. Increased ageing of the population, medical progress and unemployment and poverty tending to rise, cause the required funding to be raised over and over again.

The starting point was a 50-50 division of the social insurance cost between employers and employees. In Germany in order to relieve the employers of the expenses, employer's contributions were capped and further additional charges carried only by the employees and in the form of additional payments for medical expenses. However, this solution is irresponsible under social-ethical points of view because of the unequal distribution of income and property distribution.

The following principles should be valid for the financing of the social security:

[162] http://www.ard.de/intern/abc/-/id=1643802/nid=1643802/did=1657074/1ooe02s/index.html#abcListItem_1657074

1. **Expansion of the employer's contributions for all enterprises**
   Employer's contributions may be raised not only by those enterprises which occupy employees, but also by all enterprises. A one-sided burden of employers occupying employees raises the price of the labour cost and promotes rationalisation by restriction of jobs. So it is advisable:
   a.) to raise employer's contributions for all enterprises related to the added-value. The financial burden would thereby be reduced for labour-intensive companies, and with it the rationalisation pressure and the danger of the drift of labour-intensive manufacturing in cheap wage countries, and the total of contributions of the employers, would be higher, whilst sinking for enterprises employing many employees.
   Though, it cannot be excluded that the higher costs will be passed on to the prices. But as far as this happens, these costs would evenly spread on all products and services, not just burden the products of labour intensive companies.
   b.) For the purpose of a basic pension for everybody, all people active in the economic field should be charged social security contributions in accordance with their income. Additional private policies can be taken out for any additional medical services surpassing the basic protection.
2. **Financing of the pensions from Death Taxes**
   As already discussed, a balanced free market economy requires that inheritances are more highly taxed. Accumulation of property, (as far as it is not used, real-economically invested or donated for charitable purposes), is only economic-ethically justified for the provision of old age.
   If a person dies without having used his means for the provision for old age, after the deduction of an adequate inheritance for the descendants, the property should run into the pension scheme and support the provision for the old age of all. The inheritance tax could also be paid in real values: Real estate, mortgages, shares and thus built up a capital stock for the pension scheme. The less persons able to work to finance the pension scheme because of the population pyramid getting worse, the more capital stock revenues must fill the financial gap. In view of these yields no additional social security contributions need to be raised.

2.2 Schools and Kindergartens

Public schools and kindergartens have been financed up to now through tax means, which means everybody is burdened whether they have children or not.

To involve the citizens more in the school activities and the kindergartens, and to promote the competition between schools and kindergartens, the citizens should be obliged to a general education delivery. Besides, it should be left to them which school or kindergarten they give their fees to.

The schools and kindergartens should apply for these deliveries. That is, good schools and kindergartens will receive more means than bad ones. Of course it must be legally ensured that less qualified pupils and children are not excluded from the lessons. The schools are liable to account towards their financiers of course. Because of this accountability, and also to be optimally placed in the competition with other institutions, the economic use of the means is guaranteed.

An advisory board should be elected from those financing the schools and kindergartens, which consults the schools. They must also select a school or a kindergarten to which they want to hand over their deliveries as, just like with tax duty, citizens without children are charged with contributions for the schools and kindergartens..

As a result of the direct financing of schools and kindergartens, the citizens are integrated stronger in the questions of education and care of children up to integration problems; they are thus additionally motivated, in particular if they have already retired from employment and are prepared to give advice and private lessons, to help with childcare etc. in an honorary capacity. Thus schools and kindergartens are no more an anonymity but a matter of all, for the majority of citizens.

>>The direct taxes have to be lowered on a par with the amount of contributions. Those who cannot prove any contributions should pay more taxes than the contributions would have cost. ... Accordingly cultural facilities and colleges should be financed.<< [163]

3. Infrastructure companies

Liberals would like to reduce the role of the state in the economy to a sort of *night watchman's function*. The state should only guarantee the market rules. They demand over and over again that state enterprises have to be privatised. As an argument they state that private profit interest provides more economic efficiency. Also private enterprises would react in a more adaptable manner, and more creatively to new possibilities, than a cumbersome state bureaucracy.

These theses have a certain authorisation. However, they are not necessarily valid if the special market has no sufficient competition as it is the case, among other things, with networked traffic systems, and the energy and water supply. In these areas it easily comes to monopoly profits and a disregard of necessary investments because the population cannot defend itself. A spectacular example of it at the moment is the neglected Federal Railroad and Berlin city railroad investments and the excessive thinning out of the number of staff whereby the security at the railway stations and on the trains is also affected.

[163] Petersen (2010 a), p. 393f.

However a good long distance, and in particular urban transport infrastructure, belongs to the bases of economic and social life. If these services are offered under usual market conditions, they can become so expensive because of the monopoly position, but also for cost reasons that the general mobility desirable in itself and in particular of the lower income subscribers is limited. Then this restriction entails other necessary costs, and with it price increases and thereby the readiness to use these traffic systems is once more limited.

This trend still is strengthened by car owners who use the local traffic less and shift the infrastructure costs of the roads even moreso to less wealthy people, while public streets are financed from tax means.

So it is advisable to run the road traffic in a *corporation of public law*. However, the railway should not finance itself any more by the sales of tickets, but by a reallocation which is imposed on all citizens whether they use the railway or not. That means: those would also be charged with the traffic delivery who up to now go by car or airplane, however, they will consider under these conditions whether they would not rather go free of charge by train because they must pay the traffic delivery anyway. The general energy consumption and the air pollution could be also decreased by a stronger shifting of the traffic onto the railway system.

The amount of the transport services could be considerably increased by a general traffic delivery so that the rail services can be optimised and also win the attraction of all citizens.

The public radio companies could be a model for the organisation of public law transport services. Every household is charged with a license fee which also covers all other electronic net services.

According to the broadcasting council of the radio companies, transport services of public law should also be controlled by a traffic company supervisory board in which all socially relevant institutions are represented from the state up to trade unions and churches. Thus the public is still better integrated into the supervision of the transport services and its needs, and the purely political influence is forced back.

The state can be relieved of duties, and correspondingly of tax means to be used for these duties, through the foundation of the public law institutions for the satisfaction of collective needs which are financed directly by the citizens on a reallocation basis and according to the, in each case necessary, costs. In determining the amount of the reallocation's social aspects, such as number of children, needs etc. it could be also considered that those who are so rich that their consumption need will not be restricted by higher common reallocations, could be more heavily burdened.

The need to finance public measures by debt admission also decreases alongside it. Besides, it would be a contribution to further democratisation of the social decision-making process, because the citizens are more involved and interested in the duties to be solved.

In the general discussion, the financial requirements are underestimated for collective needs, such as traffic, energy supply, environmental protection, education and research and culture, and also for social benefits, so one is inclined to repair overextension through public expenditure cuts. I hope to have made clear how problematic expenditure cuts are, namely not only for reasons of a respectable infrastructure and the advancement of economy and society, but also for substituting missing private purchases because of the high savings rate.

As an additional aspect not to be neglected, the direct financing of public spending could include citizens more immediately in coping with social problems, and thus the democratisation of the society could be promoted.

D. Summary

Economic behaviour is determined by four kinds of motivations:

1. Procurement of the means of subsistence,
2. Status
3. Professional ethics
4. Capitalistic pursuit of profits.

These motivations flow together in the practical life up to a certain degree. The economic behavior follows different laws depending on which motivation rules.

1. Economic activity to ensure the means of subsistence

The most original form of economic activity serves the protection of maintenance and further needs. Other economic motivations are also based on the protection of maintenance.

On one hand, for the procurement of the means of subsistence, a person needs experiences and talent to utilise the natural products. For, natural products as a rule are scarce. On the other hand competitors must also be kept away from them. This last aspect should not be neglected. As in the animal kingdom, families, trunks, people, had to conquer their district and defend it.

Original power related economic activity is based on physical strength. So slaveholder's societies and feudalism originated. The conquerors appropriated the land and made the subjected inhabitants serve them. At that time the relations were internalised by the people, and recognised as given by God. So *estate-related economies* developed.

2. Estate-related economies

Market economists are inclined to look at the height of the income as only to be determined by offer and demand. However, this is only partly the case. Allowances of a king, the salaries of ministers and the remunerations of parliamentarians are only partly determined by offer and demand. Here it is simply determined what corresponds to the status of the respective holder of an office.

What a doctor earns can be different from state to state, and is directed extensively what the doctors earned up to now and what is estimated as adequate in proportion to other occupations. Attempts to change these relations and to reduce the salary level are mostly answered with furious protest.

Traditionally the salary of economic leaders was also calculated related to his status and to enable him a befitting income according to his social standing. This is not necessarily the same with all occupations. A manager must take part in far more social events and co finance them and become active in cultural, political and charitable institutions as it is expected from other professional guilds. He can fulfil his necessities of life, however, with an annual salary of €500,000 just as well as with a salary of € 1,000,000 or more. To live a befitting social standing life, the salaries must not go in to the millions and grow furthermore disproportionately.

The height of estate-related incomes is determined after what *one* usually earns in a certain position. Primarily, with the takeover of a position, it is about the social reputation. So a head of a company can earn absolutely less than his most competent distribution agent. However, in the course of the turbo capitalism and the *Shareholder Values,* the income for managers also became more and more a status symbol, and who wants to differ from others, tries to get a higher income, than that of other comparable managers.

This may be justified in single cases because of a special qualification. If one disregards the usual base level on which the special qualification is founded, however, it again becomes the graduation for other managers, so that the whole salary level will move upwards. Of course, immoderateness is no criterion for estate-oriented income. Because capitalistic thinking penetrates, all areas of life more and more, immoderateness also governs the salary claims of managers and, because of their nearness to the capital owners, even more than in other professional guilds.

If one assumes from the fact that everybody gives his best in his occupation and a manager's activity already produces big satisfaction and social esteem by itself, today's manager's salaries often stand in no relation to the provided service. No manager alone could gain such a salary. He needs the cooperation of all others in the enterprise for that. Accordingly the success would also have to be distributed broader or be spent for charitable purposes.

In general it cannot be derived from the salary amount, what a manager does for his enterprise, because then one could add to him the whole enterprise profit minus a market-customary payment of interest for the capital. But according to this criterion, the whole profit could be also added to any other key position because without him nobody would earn anything.

Also the argument that a manager must bear a higher risk would only be valid to the extent where if he also had to bear losses. Instead released managers demand higher compensatory packages, even if they have left gigantic losses in the company. Estate-related thinking also expresses itself here, interestingly however only if losses are made. If profits are made, compensations should be paid according to capitalistic criteria.

Status thinking also obviously determines the amount of the manager's salaries. Whether a good manager receives €500,000 or €5,000,000 and/or, in addition, still share options, this will not influence his management achievement, and if so, then he is not a serious manager to be respected. [164] Bonus payments

[164] See also: *Ist die Vergütung von Managern mit mehreren Millionen Euro pro Jahr wirtschaftsethisch vertretbar?* in: *Unkonventionelle* ... (I), p. 87ff.

and in particular in the form of shares, can even motivate him to prefer short-term stock exchange referring profit instead of the long-term protection of the enterprise.

What is to be regarded as an adequate manager's salary is also different from country to country. To my knowledge the highest manager's salaries were in America. Consequently the salaries of the other managers of Mercedes had to be adapted after the acquisition of Chrysler. The managers of Mercedes will not have worked more effectively afterwards.

For managers there is in no market value in the real sense, but only the trend to increase the revenues higher and higher. If it was normal for managers to earn €500,000, then it would already be an improvement if somebody got €600,000 offered for this function in another enterprise. A manager with a salary of €1,000,000 or €600,000 can hardly satisfy his needs better than if he was only earning €500,000. Still it injures his self-confidence if he is worse compensated than a colleague with whom he compares himself, that is, for him his salary is to a large extent a *status symbol*. Because the salaries are fixed by other managers, and the salaries concerning the enterprise turnover and/or profit are peanuts, there is only an *upwards open Richter Scale* for manager's salaries if social norms are not fixed for it.

Status-related economics tends to pension income which results from a property. Status-related income is based on the conviction: one does not *get* rich, one *is* rich. Status-related economics also are hardly to be founded rationally. It can be seen most clearly in the art trade if, for example, a container with a cow inlaid in spirit is purchased at an auction for many millions of dollars. Of course the motive can resonate with an art purchase to be able to resell the piece of art possibly later for a higher price. However, often it does not depend on it at all. The buyer might enjoy only the consciousness that he has generated special attention due to an unusual action, has trumped others and can call a unique artwork his property.

Really status-related action does not need to boost our own selfconfidence by such actions. One only partially acts with all status-related behavior concerning securing one's own livelihoods. If status-related behavior is reduced to own as much money as possible, or in money expressible assets, then we speak of a *capitalistic activity*. On the other side if economic behavior is motivated decisively by a professional ethics, we call it: *economic activity as profession*.

3. Economic acting as profession

An individual does not live not alone, but rather in a community, and also sees himself predominantly as a limb of the community. Communities are firstly structured in a traditional manner in respect of the sensible division of labour. The first model is where the family which is organised like in the animal kingdom mostly patriarchal and what is almost certainly owed to the relatively bigger strength of men and their assertiveness. Accordingly larger communities are also structured hierarchically.

Economic effectiveness rose with the division of labour. So within time, certain professional guilds developed. First the qualifications were transferred from the parents to the children. In the course of social development and individuation of the people, the children chose their own profession, however, more and more according to their abilities and inclinations. They wanted to earn their living with it but also wanted to serve the society. Accordingly they organised themselves in different professions with their own professional ethics and befitting social standing prices. Work as a pure means to maximise profit seemed a crime to them.

This went so far that innovations where a craftsman wanted to attain an advantage before his guild brothers, were considered unacceptable. *Peter Borscheid* writes:>> "No manual worker should conceive or invent or use something new, but everybody should follow his fellow men because of civil and brotherly love, and should do his craft without damaging his fellow men", is prescribed in the Thorner guild order of 1523.[165] Still at the end of the 17th century emperors and *Reichstag* [of the union of German states] tried to prevent the application of water mills to make the production of strings faster, because using water power would cause thousands of people and families to lose their jobs.[166] This thinking remains unchanged despite, or maybe because of, economic-liberal postulates from the 18th century. In French Amiens two manufacturers were pursued judicially in 1742 because they innovated their production and wanted to supervise and work better using equipment from a manufacture of 200 looms.[167]<<[168]

Profit maximisation as a motivation to work is almost regarded as the norm today. But the fact that this is the exception is not taken into consideration. Who becomes a tailor, shoemaker, locksmith, teacher, doctor does not choose his occupation to only just earn money. Earning his living is only viewed as natural compensation for his services to society. People also want to be realised in their occupation, and are motivated by professional ethics. Who wants to become a priest, teacher or scientist, does not aim to become a medical professional or an

---

[165] Karlheinz A. Geißler: *Die Zeiten ändern sich. Vom Umgang mit der Zeit in unterschiedlichen Epochen*, in: Aus Politik und Zeitgeschichte. Beilage zu Wochenzeitung Das Parlament vom 30.07.1999, p.5

[166] Rudolf Wendorff (1980): *Zeit und Kultur. Geschichte des Zeitbewusstseins in Europa*, Opladen, p.130.

[167] Bernard Lepetit: *Frankreich 1750-1850*, in: Mieck, Ilja (Hg.) (1993): Hdb. der europäischen Wirtschaftsund Sozialgeschichte, Vol. 4, Stuttgart, p.503

[168] Peter Borscheid: *Das Tempo-Virup. Eine Kulturgeschichte der Beschleunigung*, Campus Verlag Frankfurt/New York 2004, p.22

entrepreneur because he could earn more money through such a profession, because if he did do it he would neither reach optimal achievements nor take pleasure in his work.

This is even more valid for artists or development workers. Even an entrepreneur who develops, produces and expels certain goods, depends on his occupation, his job, his employees, even if he also develops, purchases and produces in a profit oriented manner. His work may be capitalistically structured, but his motive however, is to be an approved part of society. This changes if capitalistic monetary acquisition becomes the sole graduation of economic action.

4. Capitalistic acting

As a matter of fact a capitalist must also earn his living. However, this motive does not play the first role. For him making profit has its end in accumulating cash values and thereby power. Of course he can also acquire concrete things, such as real estate or objects of value. He estimates this, however, not because of how useful they are, but rather only because of their cash value. A capitalist founds his self-confidence not on concrete abilities and character qualities, but on the achieved financial property status. According to these criteria he also assesses others. Therefore, in the USA it is usual to judge other people by how many dollars they are worth.

Somebody with a calling carries his value in himself and in what he does. A status-related man founds his self-confidence on what social position he has, and a capitalist on his *money*.

In spite of the actual complexity of economic motivations in the usual economic theories, only capitalistic behavior is regarded as the real economic acting. It is only about the maximisation of profit expressible in money. Whether wages fall under the subsistence level in the interest of this aim, jobs are destroyed and employees are torn over and over again from out of their social connections and/or whether nature is destroyed, does not flow into economic calculations, unless the enterprises are forced by law to consider such impacts or because they would damage their reputation otherwise.

Although profit-related economic behaviour was limited originally to the capitalistic enterpriser, the western economic theory hypostatised it to be the sole motive for all economic action, and as a so-called *natural* economic motive has also corrupted the behavior of the other partners in the economic life over time. This in particular can be seen in the so-called *Shareholder's Value Doctrine* which obliges management and employees to only work for the profit maximisation of stockholders.[169]

---

[169] see: *Die schleichende Zerstörung der Wirtschaftsethik*, in: *Unkonventionelle* ...(I), p. 81ff.

Unfortunately however, only the income of the lower income subscribers should be low in line with the *Shareholder's Value Doctrine*. The higher the incomes the more the salary calculation is also determined by status considerations.

Instead of giving every young person the similar start terms according to the principle of equality, the economic start of the possession of property is determined to a large extent by feudal inheritance principles. So it is not surprising that the income and property distribution has moved, and shifts on further in favour of only a few.

This increasing movement is doubtful not only economic-ethically, but because it also destroys the economy and society. For in the extent, as income runs only to a few, these few must spend their income on consumption or investments.

From that follows:

1. all savings must be invested in a profit-oriented manner, otherwise goods remain unsold at the market, and
2. the economy must grow at the rate of expected yields of the invested capital, namely also if the mass income does not rise any more or even falls because of high rationalisation investments, and all additional income is only earned by a few.
3. The savings for which no real-economic investment possibilities are found, must be *burnt* at the capital market, so that the balance is compensated between supply and demand of goods and services.
   Economical savings are burnt by
   a.) purchase of government stocks via which the savings become economical consumption again,
   b.) fees for the finance service providers who, as experience shows, have a low savings rate with high income and
   c.) speculative forcing up of the value of real estate, shares, gold, currencies etc. and use of virtual profits for consumption purposes.
   So by speculation, unconcerned owners of real estate and stocks get even richer. If they use a part of this value increase of their property for consumption purposes, economical savings are burnt. However, this loss is only realised when the prices fall again. One thinks of American real estate owners who pledged speculative value increases of their real estate in return for loan admissions, and financed loan consumption with these.[170]

Because the monetary expansion required for capital market plays became bigger and bigger in proportion to real-economic payment processes, to the astonishment of economic theorists the expectation was no more valid than that of

[170] See: Petersen (2010 a), p. 94ff.

monetary increase must release inflation.[171] Price increases of shares are not evaluated as inflation. The monetary policy is a weighty reason that a money supply limitation was cancelled with it. So by deregulations, the scriptural currency creation possibility of the banks was also expanded.

After the breakdown of the speculation bubbles, in particular the real estate bubble in 2007/2008, the economic politicians believed they found the real cause for the ongoing crisis in the deregulations of the bank activity. Therefore nearly all economic discussions about the prevention of future crises were primarily about how the power of the banks, or as one is in habit to say of the "markets", can be adjusted that no more economic crises appear.

In these discussions the fact that excessive savings are *burnt* by the speculations and capital market plays is not taken in consideration. Depressions are thereby prevented because offered goods and services do not remain unsold.

The American central bank FED, which was and still is a forerunner with the deregulation of the banks and flooding the economy with money, has seen the danger that the economy might be strangled if not enough liquidity is made available to the capital market. The flood should and has prevented dreaded depressions; however, as the depression broke out it happened more violently.

So one should not be surprised that the efforts are ever slow in making headway in the renewed regulation of the capital market, and moreover the countries which particularly profit as finance centers from capital market services thus resist against stronger capital market controls.

Countries with an active trade balance bind excessive savings through capital export corresponding to the profit of the trade balance. The amount of the capital export will be invested or consumed in other countries. However, the indebtedness of these countries thereby rises and can cause international commercial problems, in particular if the means are used for consumption, that is, as savings are *burnt* and therefore no equivalent exists which the advances can be paid back from.

It also has to be considered to the extent that capital flows into a country, the exchange rate will rise or will be prevented to fall, thereby resulting in exports of the country becoming more expensive and imports cheaper. In particular the USA suffered, and still suffers now from it. The indebtedness of the United States thereby not only increased, but the high exchange rate also contributed to the *deindustrialisation* of the USA.

Capital streams and commercial streams will have to be administratively adjusted in a more forceful manner because of the different business development of the countries and the effects of the capital market transactions on the exchange rates, and also because no economy can exist with only high tech-industry or cheap wage manufacturing, .

---

[171] See: *Wann kommt die von Politikern und vielen Wirtschaftswissenschaftlern erwartete Inflation?* in: *Unkonventionelle* ... (I), p. 45ff.

Because the financial crisis endangers the euro zone, the overextension of single European states has determined the economic discussion since 2010. The Governments are of course responsible for the rising public indebtedness, which is more than 100 percent of the gross domestic product in many countries, in particular because due taxes were not collected as reported in Greece, and not enough tax deliveries were raised for the financing of the state expenses. So-called "debt brakes" can prevent that the public authorities adapt their income to necessary expenses, and are therefore to be welcomed.

Unfortunately however, the discussion about public indebtedness is not led thus. Rather it is assumed that the public spending is not justified by the height and must be reduced consequently. However this argument does not consider that excessive savings become economical consumption again via state loans, that is are *burnt* as savings. Instead of raising taxes and deliveries from the citizens according to their efficiency, and return the purchase power to the business circle via state expenses, the savings are taken from the citizens by state loans.

In both cases the real-economic balance is compensated in respect of supply and demand. Only in the last case the capital market is flooded with insubstantial debt papers, which are, or were, erroneously still regarded as especially crisis-resistant.

Economic theory and politics do not usually consider how savers can invest their excessive savings, or to what extent the economy must grow even faster if the states would not take the savings from savers but would instead return it to the national economy as a consumption again.[172]

The economy can only really become redeveloped through measures by which the property and income distribution becomes well-balanced again. For that purpose the old debts should be taken from the market as suggested by *debt cuts, property deliveries and a conversion of the monetary creation principles,* not least in order to prevent speculations against states and currencies too. That should be done to avert the immediate dangers threatening the economy and currencies.

So that no other potential crises develop again, the public revenues are to be adapted to the necessary expenses.

Indeed, no excessive state should originate. So non-profit interests should be separated from the state as far as possible, and be transferred to reallocation financed institutions or corporations of public law and private society-related associations and institutes. The citizens could be thereby more strongly integrated into such duties as education and cultural support and the society could further be democratised. To sum up, the duties to be solved could be characterised as: *From the liberal to the social-liberal economic system.*

---

172 See: *Was machen die Gläubiger der Staatsschulden, wenn die Staaten ihre Ausgaben reduzieren und den Anlegern somit keine Staatspapiere mehr verkaufen oder sogar bestehende Schulden zurückzahlen?* in: Unkonventionelle ... (I), p. 67ff.

Bibliography

Aristoteles: Nicomachische Ethik V, 5–8, 1130 b–1133 b 29.

Achleitner, Ann-Kristin: *Handbuch Investment Banking*, Gabler Verlag, 2002.

Borscheid, Peter: *Das Tempo-Virus. Eine Kulturgeschichte der Beschleunigung*, Campus Verlag Frankfurt/New York 2004.

Dierse, U.: *Ökonomie*, in : Hist. Wörterbuch der Philosophie Bd. 6, S. 1153.

Facebook & Co.: *Der neue Hype im Internet*, in: Rendite Das Anlagemagazin der Börsenzeitung, v. 11. September 2011, p.11.

Funck-Brentano, T., *L'économie politique patronale* = Einl. zur Neu-A. von MONTCHRESTIEN, Traicté de l'œconomie politique (Rouen 1615) (Paris 1930) I–CXVII.

Gadamer, Hans-Georg*: Hermeneutik II*, J.C.B. Mohr (Paul Siebeck) Tübingen 1990.

Geißler, Karlheinz A.: *Die Zeiten ändern sich. Vom Umgang mit der Zeit in unterschiedlichen Epochen*, in: Aus Politik und Zeitgeschichte. Beilage zu Wochenzeitung Das Parlament vom 30.07.1999, p.5.

Griechenland: *Milliardenschwere Schattenwirtschaft* ARTE Journal 11. 2010.

Griechenland: *Schmiergelder an der Tagesordnung*, in:ARTE Journal 10.2.2010.

Häußermann, Hartmut/Siebel, Walter 1995: *Dienstleistungsgesellschaften*.

Hubschmid, Maris und Henrik Mortsiefer: *„Die Gefahr sieht kleiner aus"*, in: Der Tagesspiegel, Nr. 21142, 31.10.2011, p. 16.

Justi, J. H. G.: *Die Chimäre des Gleichgewichts von Europa* (1758).

Kaiser, Stefan Spiegel Interview mit Ex-Banker und Multimillionär Harald Christ: Höhere Steuern für Vermögende, 31.08.2011,

Kreiner, Paul: Italiens Problem, in: Der Tagesspiegel Nr. 21138, 27.1.2011, S. 2

Kroszner, Randall S.; Raghuram G. Rajan: *The Role of Firewalls in Universal Banks: Evidence from Commercial Bank Securities Activities before the Glass-Steagall Act*, University of Chicago George G. Stigler Center for Study of Economy and State, Chicago, 1994.

Krug, W. T.: Art. ‹Oekonomik›, in: Handwb. der philos. Wiss. 3 (21833) 97.

Kuchenbecker, Tanja, Rolf Obertreis, Elisa Simantke: *Ein harter Schnitt*, in: Der Tagesspiegel, Nr. 21138 v. 27.10.2011, p. 2.

Laroche, E.: Hist. de la racine NEM-en grec ancien (Paris 1949) 142–144.

Lehmkuhl, Dieter, „Mitinitiator der Initiative Vermögender für eine Vermögensabgabe": *Eigentum verpflichtet!*, Gastkommentar im Tagesspiegel am 25.01.2011.

Lepetit, Bernard: *Frankreich 1750-1850*, in: Mieck, Ilja (Hg.) (1993): Hdb. der europäischen Wirtschaftsund Sozialgeschichte, Bd. 4, Stuttgart, S.503.

Maier, Claudia: *Psychisch krank in jungen Jahren*, in: Der Tagesspiegel Nr. 21 129 v. 18.10.2011, S.16.

Meier, Albrecht: *Versprochen gebrochen*, in: Der Tagesspiegel Nr. 21 120, 9.10.2011, p. 5

Obertreis, Rolf: *„Nie besser aufgestellt"*, in: Der Tagesspiegel, Nr. 21137, 26.10.2011, p. 16.

Petersen, Uwe (2010 a): *Wirtschaftsethik und Wirtschaftspolitik .Zur Überwindung der globalen Wirtschaftskrise. Von der Liberalen zur sozialliberalen Wirtschaftsordnung*, Verlag Dr. Kovac Hamburg 2010.

Petersen, Uwe: *Unkonventionelle Betrachtungsweisen zur Wirtschaftskrise, Von Haien, Heuschrecken und sonstigem Getier* (I), Verlag Peter Lang Frankfurt am Main 2011.

Petersen, Uwe: *Unkonventionelle Betrachtungsweisen zur Wirtschaftskrise II, Krankheiten des Wirtschaftssystems und Möglichkeiten und Grenzen ihrer Heilung*, Verlag Peter Lang Frankfurt am Main 2011.

Pribram, K.: *Die Idee des Gleichgewichts in der älteren nationalökon. Theorie*. Z. Volkswirtschaft, Sozialpolitik und Verwaltung 17 (1908) 1–28.

Rabe, H.: *Ökonomie*, in: Hist. Wörterbuch der Philosophie vol. 6, p. 1149.

Ricardo D.: Letters of D. Ricardo to Th. R. Malthus, hg. J. BONAR (Oxford 1887) 175; D.RICARDO, D.: *On the principles of pol. economy and taxation* (London 1817) Introduction.

Richter, Mathias: *Der Präsident der EU-Kommission schlägt eine EU-weite Finanztransaktionssteuer vor*, in: Märkische Allgemeine, 29.9.2011.

rtr: *USA schränken Spekulation mit Rohstoffen ein*, in: Der Tagesspiegel Nr. 21 131 v. 20.10.2011, p.22.

Schröder Miriam, Meier, Albrecht: *Das ABC der Schuldenkrise*, in: Der Tagesspiegel Nummer 21 119, 8.10.2011, p. 2.

Schulz, Thomas: *Die Ein-Prozent-Macht*, in: Der Spiegel Nr.43/24.10.11, p. 74ff.

Seigfried, A.: *Politische Ökonomie*, in Hist. Wb. der Philos. Bd. 6, S. 1165f.

Smith, Adam: *An inquiry into the nature and causes of the wealth of nations* (London 1776).

Smoltczyk, Alexander: *Salto mortale*, in: Der Spiegel Nr. 42/17.10.11, S. 112.

Stocker, Klaus: Management internationaler Finanz und Währungsrisiken, Gabler Verlag, 2., vollst. überarb. Aufl. 2006

U.S. Census Bureau: *Foreign Trade*, http://www.census.gov/foreign-trade/ balance/c5880.html

Walch, J. G.: Art. ‹Ö.›, in: Philos. Lex. 3 (41775) 312.

Weber, Max: *Die protestantische Ethik und der Geist des Kapitalismus, in:* Gesammelte Ausätze zur Religionssoziologie I, UTB, J.C.B. Mohr (Paul Siebeck), Tübingen, p. 17-206.

Wendorff, Rudolf (1980): *Zeit und Kultur. Geschichte des Zeitbewusstseins in Europa*, Opladen, p.130

Zeise, Lukas: *Geld der vertrackte Kern des Kapitalismus*, Papy Rossa Verlag 2010.